A Sociological Yearbook of Religion in Britain · 4

# A Sociological Yearbook
# of Religion in Britain · 4

*Edited by Michael Hill*

SCM PRESS LTD

334 01571 5

*First published 1971*
*by SCM Press Ltd*
*56 Bloomsbury Street London WC1*

© *SCM Press Ltd 1971*

*Type set by Gloucester Typesetting Co. and*
*printed in Great Britain by*
*Fletcher & Son Ltd, Norwich*

# CONTENTS

# THE CONTRIBUTORS

FRANCIS ABSALOM   Lecturer in Sociology, High Wycombe College of Technology and Art

ROBERT BUCKLE   Lecturer in Social Studies, The David Dale College, Glasgow

DAVID B. CLARK   Methodist Minister, West Greenwich

KEVIN CLEMENTS   Post-Doctoral Scholar, University of Oxford

ROBERT W. COLES   Lecturer in Sociology, University of York

MICHAEL HILL   Lecturer in Sociology, London School of Economics and Political Science

NICHOLAS KOKOSALAKIS   Lecturer in Department of Social Science, University of Liverpool

STEPHEN SHAROT   Lecturer in Department of Sociology, University of Leicester

PETER L. SISSONS   Director of the Church and Society Research Unit and Lecturer in Departments of Social Anthropology and Christian Ethics and Practical Theology in the University of Edinburgh

BRYAN S. TURNER   Probationary Lecturer in Department of Sociology, University of Aberdeen

JOHN WHITWORTH   Assistant Professor of Sociology, Simon Fraser University, Vancouver

JOHN WILSON   Assistant Professor, in Department of Sociology Duke University, Durham, North Carolina

# PREFACE

THE FOURTH edition of the Yearbook follows the general lines which David Martin so effectively established in the first three editions. There is a mixture of theoretical, empirical, historical and Commonwealth material, and as usual an attempt has been made to provide something of interest to a range of diverse but overlapping groups of readers. As before, comments and suggestions are very welcome and an attempt will be made in subsequent issues to keep to the *via media* of the sociology of religion.

A brief indication of the main areas of concern in the present edition may be helpful. John Wilson's article on the sociology of schism is a reworking of Smelser's theory of collective behaviour using the historical examples of the 1848 schism in the Plymouth Brethren, the 1827 secession of the Hicksite Quakers and the 1828 formation of the Protestant Methodists. Both social and ideological factors are analysed in each case. The article by Dr Kokosalakis on Liverpool Roman Catholics is similarly concerned with the internal strains of a religious body whose system of authority is no longer compatible with external ideological conditions.

Clements' article on the influence of New Zealand churches during the Depression presents a very different picture. In a situation in which political interpretations and remedies had been completely shattered by the impact of uncontrollable events, the Christian churches provided viable 'meanings' which were eventually taken over by radical political groups. In this case religious institutions operated as the independent variable in a process of social change. The paper by Absalom shows how the Anglo-Catholic priest was able to adopt a traditional authoritarian-paternalist role with charismatic overtones in the early stages of the movement but later found that this role was no longer available. In the following article by Sissons, evidence is given of two ways in which church members in a Scottish industrial town articulate their relationship with the wider society – either by seeing the church as an antithetical subculture set against the surrounding society or as an elite group embodying in an exemplary form the highest ideals and values of the society.

John Whitworth's study of the Bruderhof in England breaks new ground as far as the Yearbook (and any other sociological journal in this country, for that matter) is concerned. The organizational stresses which resulted from the sect's oscillation between the opposite poles of isolation and evangelization are particularly interesting. There are insights too for those who are interested in contemporary commune experiments. The following article by Hill and Turner uses a classical Weberian framework to analyse Methodism's emergence within, and eventual separation from the Church of England.

The paper by Stephen Sharot is an important contribution to the ongoing secularization debate. He defines secularization as the differentiation of religious (supernatural) from non-religious (secular) perceptions of the world and spheres of action. These concepts are applied to Anglo-Jewry which, on this definition of secularization, has always been comparatively secularized. This is the first article on Judaism to appear in the Yearbook – indeed, one of the few to be concerned with a group outside Christianity. It show show fruitful comparative research can be and it establishes a need for more material of this kind in the Yearbook.

David Clark's article completes his contribution to the previous Yearbook. His account of the various strategies and bargaining processes which were explored by a Methodist minister in an attempt to overcome 'local' resistance to 'cosmopolitan' developments is a fascinating and amusing narrative. The final article by Buckle on the Mormons is an example of how the replication of a previous survey, in this case ATV's *Television and Religion* survey, provides a valuable basis for comparison.

Bob Coles has managed to produce a supplementary bibliography of some 75 items, which should be immensely useful to anyone who, like me, finds it increasingly difficult to keep pace with the growth of the field. Together with Colin Campbell and myself, Bob has been trying to get the problem of data collection and retrieval on to an efficient and computerized basis. So far we have gone a long way towards producing what I think is called software (we have a well-designed program that copes with bibliographies) but we have not yet arranged the financing of the project. I hope that in the next issue of the Yearbook we will have something more concrete to report.

MICHAEL HILL
*The London School of Economics and Political Science*

# 1 The Sociology of Schism

## John Wilson

THE history of most of the mainstream Protestant denominations is one of repeated division. Despite this fact, few attempts have been made to go beyond particular accounts of the schismatic process to formulate any kind of theory of schism. Where the sociologist has entered this field, he has done so in search of factors important in the movement's social environment such as racial, class, or regional interests. In other words, he sees schisms as the expression of social differences rather than the doctrinal and liturgical disputes they ostensibly represent. This approach is informative because it enables us to understand the social grounding of religious conflict and it does acknowledge that schism is one of the most common ways in which new religious groups appear. However, it does not tell the full story, for it does not tell us why social conflict should lead to religious separation, simply because it does not look inside the schism-rent group to examine the tensions and strains found within.

In his attempt to develop initial generalizations in a relatively untouched field, the sociologist is often led to apply insights and perspectives gained from other areas of sociology. In the case of schism this kind of help is not readily forthcoming as the study of the schismatic process in related fields is virtually non-existent. Our understanding of fission in political parties, trade unions, formal organizations or voluntary associations is as sketchy as our knowledge of that same process in religious movements. Much of our failure to understand schism, at least in comprehensive sociological terms, is attributable, therefore, to a lack of usable models (derived either by the sociologist of religion or borrowed from practitioners in another field) with which to order the usually complex mass of facts pertaining to the schismatic process.

In what follows, an attempt will be made to apply a model of social movements to the analysis of schism. The parallel should be obvious. The religious movement in which the schism takes place is seen as the society and the schismatic group as a social movement which seeks in this case, not so much to overthrow the 'society' (although this may occur) but to withdraw. In other words, in the case of schism we observe not only the creation and intensification of conflict but its qualitative transformation into an open break. The closest parallel in the field of sociology is the social movement which seeks to withdraw from society after a period of conflict. This withdrawal may be geographical, in which case the social movement is able to divorce itself completely from its former association, or it may be social, in which case the movement, although forced to remain in the world, is not of it. It is only in the field of social movements that concerted attempts have been made to observe and understand occasions when social systems seem to be flying apart.

The adoption of this kind of perspective on schism is not, of course, new. Stark, for example, has gone so far as to say that all schisms represent in reality a political challenge to the *status quo* and should therefore be seen and explained in the same light as political revolts.[1] The model of schism which will be applied here is based upon the theory of collective behaviour developed by Neil Smelser.[2] The model will be applied to three cases of schism chosen mainly on the ground of available sociological data. These are the withdrawal of the Protestant Methodist church from Methodism in 1828; the Hicksite separation of the Quakers in 1827; and the fission of the Brethren movement into Open and Exclusive churches in 1848.[3]


*Plymouth Brethren*

In 1848 the Plymouth Brethren movement split into the Open Brethren led by Groves and the Exclusive Brethren led by Darby. In so far as Darby was the leader accepted by the majority of Brethren in the first twenty or so years of the movement's existence it is more correct to speak of the Open Brethren as the schismatic group, and they were indeed in the minority in 1848. The principal issues behind the split were doctrinal and organizational. The original doctrinal dispute was between Newton and Darby, the latter disagreeing with Newton's views on the sufferings of Christ. The organizational dispute concerned the question of open communion – the freedom with which new members were to be allowed to break bread with the Brethren. Darby took a much more rigorous view of the requirements and combined this with an inclination towards more centralized government.

## Hicksite Quakers

The Hicksite body of Quakers originated in a split in the Philadelphia yearly meeting of 1827. Although at first a local affair, the split soon spread until it involved most of the Friends in America.

## Protestant Methodists

In discussing the numerous divisions which occurred in Methodism during the nineteenth century, Currie distinguishes between secessions and offshoots. The latter were generally revivalist in emphasis and developed a mass following around very few ex-Wesleyans. The Primitive Methodist schism would be an example of this kind. The secessionist groups were 'almost entirely composed of ex-Wesleyans and did little recruiting in the outside world'[4] and thus resemble more accurately the customary definition of a schismatic group. An example of a church formed in this way is the Protestant Methodist Church.

The Protestant Methodist Church has its origins in a Revivalist Party based in Leeds and led, first by William Bramwell, from about 1803, and later by a layman, James Sigston. Eckett, another prominent layman in Yorkshire Methodism, was also active in the party. The broad objective of the party was the restoration of the pristine principles of Wesleyanism. The party became a separate sect in 1828 when about 3,000 members left the parent church over a dispute concerning the installation of an organ in the Brunswick Chapel in Leeds.

Incidentally, although our main attention will be directed at the structure of each movement, it is no accident that each of these schisms took place in the nineteenth century and that few comparable examples can be found in the twentieth. There are some grounds for believing that schisms are much more common in eras of religious expansion and optimism and the reverse process, ecumenicism, more common in an age of declining activism.[5]

The model on which Smelser's theory of collective behaviour is based is intended to suggest the necessary and sufficient conditions for the occurrence of schism. As will be seen, the model is not perfect, and stands in need of considerable refinement, but in its basic rudiments it would seem to be a useful beginning to the study of fission and will in any case only be refined by repeated application. The concepts and rationale of the model are taken from the work of Talcott

Parsons. Only the barest outlines of the model and its derivation from that source can be indicated here.

Parsons, in an attempt to construct a model describing the structure of social action, takes as his basic unit the social actor. This social actor is typically conceived as pursuing goals in a situation over which he has only partial control according to means which have to a large degree been dictated by his social environment. Thus, to Parsons, social action is composed of an actor, his ends, the norms which determine his method of achieving them, and the environment.

Smelser takes over this model but seeks to apply it to a higher level of generality, taking as his focus, not the individual social actor but the social structure, or an association of social actors. Transposed to this higher level the major components become values, norms, roles and situational facilities. The purpose of this attempt to analyse the components of social structure is to indicate on a general basis those problem areas which need to be covered before a total sociological explanation can be said to have been given. In other words, social structures have four components which have to be taken into account in trying to understand a pattern of activities. Some of these components, according to the model, are more important because they are more general. Thus values stand at a higher level of 'control' over our behaviour; they are more important to us than situational facilities. A change in values will effect a change in all the components below it in the hierarchy of control, but the reverse does not apply.

Smelser, in attempting to explain the outbreak of all forms of collective behaviour, suggests a set of determinants which, in combination, comprise the necessary and sufficient conditions for the occurrence of particular episodes. As we shall see, some of these determinants are expressed in terms of the conceptual scheme put forward by Parsons. These determinants are: structural conduciveness, structural strain, mobilizing agent, precipitating factor and social control. One determinant, that of generalized belief, will be omitted in this application of the model. To Smelser, the mobilizing function performed by the generalized belief is probably the most important in the whole process of social movement emergence. It is omitted here in the belief that, as described by Smelser, schismatic groups do not withdraw on the basis of a generalized belief but do so on quite 'rational' grounds. There are a few signs of the short-circuiting of thinking or the extravagant promises and hopes in the case of schisms which Smelser suggests we always find in social movements. This is not to say that there is no mobilizing belief, only that the belief does not exhibit qualities different from the kinds of thinking current in the parent group, except of course for the substantive differences involved in the dispute.

The keystone of the model is the concept of structural strain. For present purposes strain is defined as a disjuncture between norms and values or between roles and norms. The model is based on the assumption that, in the hierarchy of control in any system, values are paramount, that norms provide the needed specification of means and that there is a tendency towards attaining and sustaining a 'fit' between values and norms. Similarly, the assumption is made that, although norms provide us with general guidance, in our day-to-day life, we specifically follow role requirements and that these role requirements tend towards some kind of 'fit' with the social norms. Put simply, strain describes a situation where accepted norms are not fully appropriate to the system's values. Most often this manifests itself in a sense of uneasiness, frustration, or disorientation, as a set of values continue to be espoused, meaningful commitment to which is inhibited by the social rules which one is expected to follow.

It is suggested here that norm-value strain is at the core of all cases of schism. It is true, of course, that structures consist of patterns made by people acting and we should not lose sight of the fact that these tensions we describe in terms of structural strain are those experienced by the members of the movement in feelings of frustration, anomia and anger. We should also not lose sight of the fact that although we described the 'faults' of the structure in terms of conflicting norms and values these faults are embodied in people living different life styles. Thus to describe the tensions leading up to schism as structural strain is not to ignore the fact that basic weaknesses in the system are seized upon, or are reflected in the social bases and alignments of the different parties. Behind all cases of schism we find different social categories with different interests and perspectives. Most often these are class issues – but racial, regional and sexual differences are potent divisive agents as well. Our analysis of strain should thus be carried on at two levels which complement each other – the one describing the strains of the system, the other describing the personal tensions and feuds which give these strains flesh and blood.

A schismatic group is a movement which has its origins in a dispute over norms and allegations that the main group has departed from those implicated in the values of the original movement. For economic or political reasons, a minority group comes to feel that departures from norms are so fundamental that they impair the movement's chances of obtaining its goals, and decides to withdraw from the parent group as a way of preserving the pristine values of the movement. The normative conflict thus escalates to a conflict over values but one which, in the case of schism, does not result in an attempt to overthrow the existing authorities in the group but which seeks to withdraw.

The concept of structural strain is a useful tool for analysing the location of tensions within a movement, but we should not suppose that systems are normally in harmony and thus without strain. In fact, both in social movements and the wider society strain is endemic, mainly in the form of conflicting interests, normative ambiguity, inadequate socialization and so on. Most important for the purposes of the study of schism, strain results from the fact that although values stand as legitimations of normative patterns these values, because of their generality, are always sufficiently vague to warrant the adoption of a variety of means of achieving them. There will always be at best uncertainty and at worst open conflict over the specific patterns of behaviour involved in commitment to a set of values.

Religious movements are ideological phenomena, with a set of more or less comprehensive values, but they share the same tenuous link between values and norms as is found in the wider society. Thus, in the continual debate as to what is the right form of association, or what is the right position of the ministry, nobody can win. In all religious movements there is a fund of issues over which conflict can legitimately take place. It is not sufficient, then, to point to the doctrinal disputes, or to the underlying social differences in cases of schism. We must look also at strains inherent in the movement which these other factors may only exacerbate.

In the case of the Brethren schism, the source of strain was the movement by the group away from the original normative patterns while commitment was still being professed to the original values. All Brethren seemed to agree that the original purpose of the movement had been to demonstrate the unity of Christian believers and witness against what they thought to be the errors of the established churches. But as the number of assemblies began to grow, pressures increased to establish some form of self-definition, thus challenging the notion of open communion. Expansion also increased the pressure towards some kind of central organization which could co-ordinate the activities of the various assemblies and this, too, was a challenge to the original anti-sectarian stance of the movement. By the 1830s, Darby had begun to agitate for some kind of pre-requisites for admission to the movement and the establishment of a metro-politan organization. Groves openly accused him of departing from the original principles of the group, and although Darby returned these charges in kind, there seems little doubt that for some Brethren, the movement seemed to have moved in terms of its normative pat-terns away from the implicit prescriptions of its foundation values, and that Darby 'had changed, if not his conscious principles, at least his method of putting them into practice'.[6]

The important point here is that this strain was implicit in the movement from the beginning and members probably entered the movement on different premises – that is, with different assumptions as to just which normative patterns were implied by the set of values on which they all agreed. For example, there seems to have existed from the time that Brethrenism began to spread two distinct attitudes towards the correctness of the establishment of supra-assembly or-ganization. By 1838 an associated but additional and exacerbating conflict over just which set of rules concerning the admission and regulation of members could be legitimately derived from the values had arisen. Some Brethren found themselves unable to live with the uncertainties created by the very openness of the early movement and sought to impose some necessary truths on the society. For others in the movement, such a move meant the sacrifice of the original prin-ciples of the group and was firmly resisted.

Added to these strains was the fact that, from the very beginning, Darby's leadership, although accepted in Ireland, London and the Continent (where the movement was known by his name), was re-jected in the West Country where Newton was the most prominent of the Brethren. Darby never managed to exercise any control over the West Country Brethren and it was, of course, they who formed the basis of the 1848 schism.

In the case of the Methodist schism which took place in 1828, the strain had two sources; the departure of the movement away from its legitimated norms and the blockage of mobility among laymen. As Currie points out, the first source of strain had been intensifying in the movement for some time. In fact, it could be said that it was present from the beginning, since Wesley's message was ambiguous enough to recruit members on entirely different bases. Wesley himself regarded the connexion as a means of binding the imperfect in one body which, largely through his own instrumentality, would effect their attainment of a state of 'perfection'. Others, who accepted Wesley's theology no less enthusiastically, saw no such justification for an extensive administrative machinery, much less the autocratic leadership practised by Wesley. Thus from the beginning, Wesley had incomplete control over different interpretations of his own message (although he did exercise strict discipline when such differences became troublesome). For many in the movement, the virtue of the association lay in its democracy. At most they were prepared to admit an advisory national organization or some means of facilitating a stronger chapel helping a weaker one.

Over time, these initial tensions were exacerbated by both the expansion of the movement and the pressing need for some kind of centralization, and by the increasing wealth of many Methodists. As Currie points out, the Methodists in the nineteenth century began to divide *de facto* if not *de jure* into wealthy Conference men and the rank and file seeking reform.

The second source of strain was the tension that existed between laymen and professional personnel. Even observers within the movement itself could see that the conflict between value promises and normative actuality had created a great deal of frustration and discontent in the movement. James Stacey, writing in 1862 of the divisions in Methodism, remarked that

> Such divisions are sure to recur under a system which fosters the popular element as Methodism does, training it to every sphere of religious activity up to the very highest, yet denying it all share in those legislative acts for which in this very training a certain preparation is given.[7]

An interesting possibility suggested by this observation is that the often remarked process whereby lower class groups who are denied secular channels of advancement and shift into the religious sphere to find power and status there, might often in fact be reversed. That is, members of religious movements, trained to religious leadership and the assumption of responsibilities, but prevented from assuming these by the blockage of opportunities at the top, might depart the group to find advancement in the secular sphere – for instance, in a trade union or a political party.

Whether or not this is true, there seems to be little doubt that much of the conflict in Methodism in the years prior to the 1828 schism was

the result of the fact that Wesley, in training a vast army of lay officials and yet excluding them from positions of power, was creating at
the same time a permanently discontented class. For example, laymen
thought they should have at least equal control over the chapels they
built and paid for. The schism of 1828 gained a great deal of impetus
from a struggle for power based upon competing claims to the same
source of legitimacy, namely, the teachings of Wesley.

Strain in the case of the Hicksite schism reflected the departure of
the movement from the norms implicated in the movement's values.
Isichei describes the development of oligarchy and its consequences
in the following terms:

> Like most sects, Quakerism began partly as a protest against hierarchy and
> professionalisation in religious groups, with the affirmation that all believers
> were equal, for all were held to be equally close to God, and likely to receive
> His enlightenment. By adopting the practice of recording ministers, they ac-
> cepted the principle of differential status within the group whilst rejecting the
> notion of payment for the services, and creating an unofficial oligarchy of the
> well-to-do. Because this oligarchy was unofficial, it could not be replaced,
> blamed for mistakes, or even officially criticised.[8]

The Hicksite party saw the movement's development of centralized
organization and an oligarchic leadership as a radical departure from
the original principles of the movement. As Doherty demonstrates,
the two parties represented on the Hicksite side an amalgamation of
liberals concerned about freedom of choice and conservative sectarians concerned about unmediated contact with the Spirit, and on
the Orthodox side a party of wealthy city-based Quakers, seeking to
move the church in the direction of accommodation and respectability.

The concept of strain in each case describes a condition which gives
rise to feelings of frustration and anger as well as puzzlement. But if
strain is ubiquitous then to a large extent such feelings are endemic in
all social movements. Obviously, a condition of strain is a necessary
factor in the occurrence of schism but hardly a sufficient one. Strain
must be combined with other factors for it to become operative in
our model. Although strain describes a conflict-producing situation,
it does not explain why factions form or schisms occur. To help
explain why discontent is allowed expression and crystallization and
yet excluded from resolution within the movement itself, we must
look at the determinant Smelser calls structural conduciveness. In its
application to total societies, this concept is intended to describe
those conditions which are most conducive in both negative and positive ways, for the formation of dissident groups which decide to move

outside the normal channels of protest. At whatever level we operate, we cannot hope to establish a finite list of these factors because in order to do so, we would have to satisfy ourselves that, for instance, all possible avenues for legal agitation had been described, or all means of communication had been covered. Instead, this part of the model is intended to direct our attention to possible structural determinants of the kind of protest to which discontent will lead. Because of the importance of this factor for the occurrence of schism, and because in the analysis of schism these kinds of factors have often been ignored, it might be as well to pay some attention to the kinds of structural features being referred to here and the kinds of hypotheses the model suggests concerning them.

Obviously, to the extent that conflict and schism are related, factors such as social differences in religious movements are important for the study of schism, but the qualitative extension of conflict such that one or both parties are prepared to rupture previously highly valued consensuses, requires a structure that is susceptible to easy fragmentation. To look at it another way, we can ask whether or not all religious movements are equally equipped to handle the disagreements over goals and means which are typical of human organizations. Based to some extent on empirical generalization, the following are suggested as some of the most important categories in terms of which structural conduciveness can be conceived.

(i) Schism is essentially a group phenomenon, for it involves the coalescence of personal dissatisfaction into a dissenting clique or faction and its subsequent withdrawal. It would seem likely therefore that schism is more probable where clique formation is easy. This in turn is more likely where solidarity ties such as kinship or community obligations compete with the ideological demands of the movement for the primary allegiance of members. It is noteworthy that totalitarian movements, as if in recognition of this danger, seek to eradicate solidarity ties which might compete with the movement itself by demanding total personal commitment to their aims and organization. Thus, one consequence of non-segmental participation is that the groups around which schismatic formations may accrete are absent.

(ii) It would seem likely that the aspect of organizational centralization is important as a structural determinant of schism. It is suggested that schism is more likely, not so much where a movement is highly decentralized, but where a movement falls at either extreme end of this continuum. In other words, groups are more prone to schism which are both highly centralized such that no decision-making powers are invested in the lower participants or regions at all, and highly decentralized such that no organization has real responsibility for co-ordination and integration, and differences can easily rupture the movement. This might help explain why schisms have occurred quite frequently in both centralized and de-centralized movements and yet in each case the *issue* of centralization has been important in the debate.

(iii) Nyomarkay has suggested that the type of authority legitimation is an important determinant of schism. Briefly put, his thesis is that schisms are more likely in ideologically legitimated movements than in those with a charismatic leader, the reasoning being that the charismatic leader is the prize for which the factions fight.

> The source of authority, or the kind of legitimacy, is relevant to the nature of factionalism because, as the focus of group cohesion, it becomes the object not the subject of factional conflict. Be it charismatic leader or the ideology, the source of authority is the prize for which factions compete. The task of factions is to attain legitimacy by identifying themselves with the source of authority. Should a faction fail in this endeavour, the members of the group will regard it as illegitimate, and it will either wither away for lack of support or split the movement and establish itself as an independent group.[9]

This last is possible only where the leader bases his claim to legitimacy on his proximity to or knowledge of the dominant values, because in this case the specific group can be departed from without surrendering proximity to the ideology. In addition, where factions constantly appeal to the dogma in disputes, conflict is constantly being raised to the highest level and theoretical issues being generated.

(iv) In some movements, the organization itself takes on a sacred aspect. It is likely that, where this is the case, the discontented will be less willing to leave the group than to try to reform it. Religious organizations are regarded either in pragmatic terms as a rational expedient, or in sacred terms as themselves part of the movement's message. The step from conflict to schism is thus partly dependent on the extent to which the parent community – not just its message – is seen as ideologically prescribed. Schism is more likely where a group comes to feel that its basic values are being threatened and at the same time believes the organization to be an artifice only.

(v) An important structural determinant of schism is the attitude taken towards the movement's ideology. Although we refer here to the aspect of dogmatism in religious groups, it is not suggested that either dogmatism or a lack of it is the more conducive to schism. In fact, we find just as many cases of schism in either type. It is suggested that both where there is extreme dogmatism, such that all innovation is heresy, and where there is a completely open truth, such that anyone can claim to have revealed it, schism is more likely.

(vi) Conflict is endemic in religious groups, but movements differ in the extent to which they prepare for it. It is suggested that in groups which do not institutionalize methods for resolving conflict, schism is more likely on the grounds that, if inevitable schism is ignored, it tends to intensify and broaden its base, extending perhaps from normative conflict to a challenge to basic values.

(vii) Finally, we refer to absence of channels for the expression of grievances. In Smelser's terms, this unavailability has three main aspects:

(a) The aggrieved group in question does not possess facilities whereby they may reconstitute the social situation; such a group ranks low on wealth, power, prestige, or access to means of communication. (b) The aggrieved group is prevented from expressing hostility that will punish some person or group considered responsible for the disturbing state of affairs. (c) The aggrieved group cannot modify the normative structure or cannot influence those who have the power to do so.[10]

This list of structurally conducive factors is probably far from complete and no prior assumptions can be made about how these various factors might be combined, or what the consequences for schism might be for particular combinations. It does, however, provide a partial checklist against which to measure the social structure of any particular social movement.

The Brethren movement from the very outset had been held together not so much by formal organizations but by influential personalities. Throughout the first twenty years of its existence, Brethrenism resembled more a loose congeries of followings of leaders in localities than a united movement. Newton of Plymouth is probably the best example of just such a leader. Thus from the very outset the movement depended a great deal on the bonds of the leader-follower relationship for its unity. The organization, to the extent that it existed at all, was highly decentralized. As far as the ideology was concerned, far from being dogmatic, the teachings of the movement were thought to be open to continued revision and development – in fact, such development was expected. In other words, one of the principal tenets of the values of the movement at the outset was that the teachings were still unfolding. The impetus of this openness, together with the importance of the local leader, was very conducive to schism. Under the foundations values, members were not isolated from non-members and the resulting heterogeneity created a great number of doctrinal disputes within the movement.

It is well known that the Methodist movement under both Wesley and Bunting was highly autocratic and centralized. Probably the main structural feature tending towards schism, however, was Wesley's use of Arminian theology to show that all could achieve the Methodist goal of perfection. Wesley thereby set up a crucial ambiguity which provided the rationale for conflict and schism throughout the dynamic period of Methodism. In Currie's words:

> ... the Arminian promise of spiritual progression for all might also suggest that achievement of perfection did not depend on obedience to ecclesiastical authority. Wesley condemned and punished deviancy but this theology could justify deviance.[11]

Added to this were the peculiar parallel structures the movement developed, which meant that the movement as a whole was highly centralized through Conference – a kind of benevolent despotism under Wesley – and yet possessed a substructure based on the chapel which, Currie suggests, Wesley knew little of but which usually provided the main source of recruitment and integration into Methodism. There existed in Methodism, right from the earliest times, a strong sentiment of chapel community loyalty which, financially autonomous, provided a basis for protest and schism.

A further structural factor conducive to schism was the pragmatic style of leadership developed by the movement on the death of Wesley. This meant, first of all, that the binding ties of Wesley's charisma were lost – neither Coke nor Bunting gained this status – and that, second, a vacuum of legitimate power, caused by Wesley's failure to provide guidance on the location of power after his death, was created, thus opening the way for strong competing claims to power.

There were three main structural factors in Quakerism that help explain the occurrence of the Hicksite schism. First the doctrine of the Inner Light which, in its extreme form, permitted a totally undogmatic ideology and a totally unmediated relationship between the believer and the divine. Second, a highly decentralized form of organization. Third, a lack of any institutionalized method of resolving conflict.

Although Quakers believed that the Light would be given to each believer, in practice a kind of group mysticism was practised whereby the sense of the meeting was taken after moments of silent prayer. Doherty and Isichei claim that such a device of decision making was not only oligarchic but also meant that important issues were ignored, suppressed or handled arbitrarily. The discrepancy between formal and actual power had created a great deal of confusion as to the true nature and locus of authority in the group – at least until the schismatic process was well under way.

The components of the model so far adumbrated are of a very general kind. Structural conduciveness, although not to be interpreted too 'passively', is chiefly a permissive factor, while the condition of strain can lead to a number of responses and, what is more important, exist as a chronic condition without necessarily leading to schism. The model thus offers little assistance in the search for the specific antecedent conditions of schism. Two other components of the models suggested by Smelser perform this function, the first by pointing to the precipitating factor and the second to the agent of mobilization.

The first provides a stimulus and excuse for direct action by symbolizing and perhaps intensifying the issues of conflict.Thus the precipitating factor, although in a sense random in so far as many incidents like it have not been seized upon as 'the last straw' or 'typical', bears an important and predictable symbolic relationship to the strains underlying the conflict. In other words, although there is no predicting just which incident – a speech, a decision, an expulsion, an event – will perform the triggering function, we can predict that something of this kind will be necessary to crystallize the issues and stimulate people to action.

In the case of the Open schism from Brethrenism, there were two precipitating factors which performed the function of defining the situation as one of irreconcilable conflict. The first was the visit of Darby to Plymouth in 1845 when he took the initiative in forcing a division by making public charges against Newton and attributing the latter's actions to the Devil. The second was the Bethesda Circular banning all communion with Bethesda's associated assemblies. '. . . Those who conformed to it became the Exclusive party, while those who rejected it or ignored it became the Open Brethren.'[12] This circular, like so many other precipitating factors, marked a point of no return in the dispute. To the Open Party it represented, both in its objects and in itself, so fundamental a normative change that the pristine values of the group were threatened.

The precipitating factor in the Protestant Methodist schism was the decision of the District meeting to forbid the installation of an organ by the Brunswick Chapel. To the District meeting, the debate over the organ represented in microcosm the general trend being experienced throughout the movement and Bunting's overthrow of its own decision on the rightness of the installation confirmed this.

The Hicksite schism had no clear triggering incident, unless we take the establishment by Hicks of a rival Yearly Meeting in Philadelphia in 1827. This certainly marked something of a point of no return for a party which had been in more or less open conflict over a period of years. In fact, Hicks' speeches between about 1820 and 1827 can be seen as one long series of precipitating factors.

The concept of mobilizing agent refers to the role played by, in most cases, a leader, in actually organizing the dissident group and defining its belief system. Such an agent is necessary before the diffuse frustrations and varied objectives of the dissidents can become effective for group action. The leader, by his own example, by his teachings, or by the strength of his own personality energizes the people into revolt. We should be careful, though, not to interpret all schisms as struggles for power between ambitious people, nor should we be blind to the important role played by outstanding figures in the transformation of a conflict group into a schismatic one.

The parties to the Brethren schism were undoubtedly mobilized by the outstanding personalities in the movement. The dissident group was led first by Groves, who was the most prescient observer of the changes going on in the movement and is claimed by the Open Brethren church today as its founder; then, after Groves' departure for missionary work in India, by Newton, who used his power base in Plymouth to challenge Darby's leadership. After Darby had taken up Newton's challenge in 1845 both leaders invited leading Brethren from various parts of the country to hear their side of the story. Although the schism had its origins in 1845 it was not really consummated until 1848. In the meantime Newton had left the Brethren movement altogether and the leadership of the Open Party had been taken over by the assembly at Bethesda, Bristol, which was headed by Muller. The schism of 1848 was in effect a clash between Darby and the Bethesda assembly. It was to Muller and his group that the Open Brethren turned when faced with the ultimatum of the Circular of 1848.

The Leeds Methodist schism, like many others, had its origins in a party within the movement. In this case it was the Revivalist party which had been formed as long ago as 1802 by William Bramwell. The effective mobilizer of the Protestant Methodist schism which arose from this party was a layman, James Sigston. It was he who organized the meeting to oppose the decision made by Bunting about the Brunswick organ. However, although his role was a significant one, it does seem rather that the main basis of solidarity among the dissident group and something which gave them a ready organizational base was the District meeting of which they were a part.

The Quaker schism of 1828 was undoubtedly mobilized by Elias Hicks, a 'prophet of the past'[13] who had for some years prior to the actual break been agitating for the retention of the traditional elements of Quakerism. It would be wrong, however, to attribute too much influence to Hicks himself. Although he was an inspiring leader, the schismatic group was united more in what it opposed than in what it proposed – a fact attested to by the frequent schisms among the Hicksites after the break. It is probable, none the less, that without Hicks the schism would not have taken place at the time and in the way it did.

The final ingredient in the model is what Smelser calls 'the forces of social control'. Smelser refers here to those authorities which play a part in defining the social position of the group and which have the power of discipline over the group. The concept is deliberately vague so as to incorporate informal sources of social pressure – as in lynching – as well as the control exercised by the formal authorities.

In attempting to apply Smelser's model to the origin of social movements it has become obvious that in fact the component of forces of social control is properly something that affects the nature of the movement once it has been formed, and cannot be considered part of its etiology. If we consider the action of the authorities to have been important before the movement has actually emerged, then it might be more correct to call this an aspect of structural strain or structural conduciveness. Most of these difficulties stem from the ambiguous nature of the movement's beginning. We often have some trouble in deciding just when a movement began, and the more difficult this decision the harder it is to decide what is really the cause since, naturally, these factors must be present first.

In the case of schism this problem does not really exist, as there are usually obvious indications of when the schism started. This is not to say that schisms are not a process, for they may be the culmination of a long period during which tensions are built up. The same is invariably true for social movements. In the analysis of schism the factor of social control is of special importance. Under this heading we wish to examine the part played by the attitudes taken by the parent church to the proposals and activities of dissidents. We must ask what responses were typically made to the expression of dissident views and how the authorities responded to the overtures of a minority leader; whether or not their reaction fanned the flames of discontent and determination to secede or whether conciliation was attempted.

Only by bringing into account the part played by the forces of social control can we properly appreciate the dialectical nature of the schismatic process and the way in which schisms grow through the exacerbation of conflict between authorities and the minority group. We must also ask whether it is not so much a firm stand or a position of weakness which creates schism as vacillation on the part of the authorities. That is, it may be the case that schisms rarely happen when authority figures are powerful enough to stifle dissent when it occurs, or so weak that no real forces of social control in a formal sense can be said to exist. Rather they happen when the group in power fails to exercise it, or when there is no clear definition of who has authority or when the authorities fail to exercise their power with conviction and consistency. The result of this last tendency, which would parallel findings made in the field of social movements, would be erratic reformism which is worse than no reform at all in that it has the consequence of alternately raising and dashing the hopes of the minority. They are thus prompted to not only a firmer conviction of their own viewpoint, but a desperation with the system as such and a desire to withdraw from it. If the forces of social control are strong enough to withstand demands for reform and yet too weak to be resolute, then schism is likely. Where the authorities are very weak then the dissidents are less likely to be prompted to withdraw but encouraged to reform the system itself.

The Brethren movement, as is probably the case with many other empirical instances, suggests that the usual conception of the forces of social control, connoting as it does legitimate authority, or at least some recognized focus of authority, may be inapplicable in the case of some schisms. The Brethren movement had no recognized specific, vertically-operating forces of social control, and the conflict represented more a debate between equals than the dissent of a minority group – as is often the case where social control is diffused and operating horizontally. If we take weight of numbers and the prominence of the leader, the Exclusivists represented the authorities but they did not in an objective sense represent the original purposes of the group. During the 1830s and 1840s Darby was the leader of a movement which shunned leadership. His purpose as an agent of social control was to try to increase his own power and to bring the conflict to the rank and file. In many ways, his actions can be said to have brought about the schism by reflecting a determination not to tolerate dissent within the movement. It is hardly likely that the Open Party, with its philosophy of open communion, would have forced a schism over doctrinal issues.

The forces of social control in Methodism were very clearly defined in the person of Jabez Bunting, whose autocratic views are well known. From the time that he gained power, Bunting determined to exercise firm control over the movement, frequently being prepared to override the constitution to get his way. Bunting is said to have looked upon the Leeds case as an opportunity to teach the long-rebellious Leeds District Meeting a lesson, and there can be little doubt that his tactics in this affair and his determination not to compromise, together with the long-standing personal animosities he created, were very significant factors in the occurrence of the schism of 1828, and the determination which the Protestant Methodist Church displayed from the outset to remain outside the Wesleyan denomination.

In Quakerism, the forces of social control, as the structure and ideology of the movement would suggest, were rather poorly defined, but as must have been the case in many other schisms, the dissident groups did a great deal to help define what was orthodox where no definition existed before. The defenders of the Orthodox position were very sensitive to Hicks' charges, and although Orthodox sentiment antedated the beginnings of the antagonism between Hicks and the Elders in 1819, the Orthodox protagonists were not well organized. Doherty suggest that Hicks, besides mobilizing his own group, also forced the Orthodox party, who were in nominal control of the movement, to 'think through their ideas and to organize in order to perpetuate their influence'.[14] Once established, however, these authorities, apart from disharmonizing personal attacks on Hicks, did not press issues which would have exacerbated the conflict. This is a case of authorities who, although they did little to appease the dissidents, did little to push them out either.

The discussion of the impact of the forces of social control brings us full circle in the analysis of the schismatic process, but the way in which the components of the model are combined ought to be made more explicit. It is suggested here that schism can be described in terms of a natural sequence of stages, each of which is dependent on the occurrence of the preceding stage. The ordering of the components, instead of being temporal, is logical – in terms of social generality. So the components, when ordered – structural conduciveness, structural strain, precipitating factor, mobilizing agent and forces of social control – describe a progression of increasing specificity such that the activation of each determines the scope and effectiveness of the next. In other words, although a stage sequence can be discerned, this is not a sequence in which the first stage brings about the condition known as the second stage, and so on, but the first stage activates the second, or the third defines the boundaries in which the fourth, which may already be in existence, can become operative. Thus the type of strain determines the kind of symbolization important in the precipitating factor.

Thus the linkage in the model is what Smelser calls 'value added'. It is not intended by the use of this concept to overstress the 'linearity' of the model. What needs stressing in fact is that the components of the model comprise a system, the parts of which are in constant interaction. We see this most clearly in the part played by the forces of social control, but it can also happen that, for instance, the mobilizing agent does not passively adopt the condition of strain but 'reacts back' upon it so to speak by reinterpreting it. These are interrelations about which we know very little at present, but which will be elucidated by extensive use of the model. Thus when we trace through the processes of schism, we may refer back to a time before the generalized belief has become current for the actual occurrence of the precipitating factors – which now becomes reinterpreted in the light of the ideology.

## NOTES

1. Werner Stark, *The Sociology of Religion*, Vol. II 'Sectarian Religion', Routledge & Kegan Paul 1967, p. 51.

2. Neil Smelser, *Theory of Collective Behaviour*, Routledge & Kegan Paul 1962.

3. Historical data is drawn from: Robert Currie, *Methodism Divided: A Study in the Sociology of Ecumenicalism*, Faber & Faber 1968; Robert Doherty, *The Hicksite Separation: A Sociological Analysis of Religious Schism in Early Nineteenth-Century America*, Rutgers University Press, New Brunswick 1967; Bryan R.

Wilson (ed.), *Patterns of Sectarianism: Organization and Ideology in Religious Movements*, Heinemann 1967.

4. Currie, op. cit., p. 54.

5. Bryan R. Wilson, *Religion in Secular Society*, Watts & Co. 1966, pp. 157–9.

6. Peter Embley, 'The Early Development of the Plymouth Brethren' in *Patterns of Sectarianism*, p. 225.

7. Currie, op. cit., p. 51.

8. Elizabeth Isichei, 'Organization and Power in the Society of Friends, 1852–59' in *Patterns of Sectarianism*, p. 209.

9. J. Nyomarkay, *Charisma and Factionalism in the Nazi Party*, OUP 1967, p. 4.

10. Smelser, op. cit., p. 325.

11. Currie, op. cit., p. 20.

12. Embley, op. cit., p. 240.

13. Doherty, op. cit., p. 27.

14. Doherty, op. cit., p. 75.

# 2 Aspects of Conflict between the Structure of Authority and the Beliefs of the Laity in the Roman Catholic Church

*N. Kokosalakis*

### Introduction

THE post-war Sociology of Religion in Britain has paid a negligible amount of attention to the study of doctrine and to problems of religious ideology as a whole.[1] As a consequence, the question of authority within religious institutions has not, even remotely, been considered with the seriousness with which the great fathers of sociology encountered the problem.[2] The reluctance of many sociologists to deal with questions of values and the structures of authority and meaning in religious institutions derives mainly from the lack of a profounder theoretical foundation and/or an adequate methodology to cope with the difficulties which these questions imply. If we are, however, to understand contemporary religious life along with all the conflicts which are embodied in religious institutions at present, it is imperative that the whole question of the ideological structure of these institutions *vis-à-vis* the beliefs of the laity be seriously examined. Especially within the Roman Catholic Church, this seems to be an outstanding question to which some attention has, already, been paid at a theoretical level.[3] In this essay, it is my intention to illustrate some of the conflicts which exist between the formal teaching and practices (and this is chiefly what is meant by 'the structure of authority') of the Roman Catholic Church and the current beliefs and loyalties of the lay members of this institution.[4]

There are two main hypotheses examined in this article.

(*a*) That there is a great disparity between the structure of authority and actual loyalty to this authority by the members of this religious body.

(*b*) That the gap is much wider and the conflict much more acutely felt by those who have been brought up and educated in the post-war society than the pre-war generations.

### Some historical factors

By and large, Liverpool Roman Catholicism has been somewhat different from that of the rest of the country in the last 150 years. The majority of the Roman Catholic population emigrated to Liverpool from Ireland during the middle and latter part of the nineteenth century. Poverty-stricken, unskilled and with very poor or no education, the Irish came pouring into Liverpool, sometimes many hundreds a day.[5] The socio-economic status of these Roman Catholics, therefore, throughout the nineteenth and for a good part of the twentieth century had been that of the underprivileged and disinherited citizen.

Immigrants are normally discriminated against in some way or other but in the case of Irish Roman Catholics in Liverpool it was not only a case of discrimination but also severe deprivation and a constant struggle for survival. This was especially true during the second half of the nineteenth century when most of Liverpool's Roman Catholics had to fight for their existence against factors such as severe poverty, illness, unemployment, social discrimination and above all, religious bigotry.

The organized Orange Lodge had launched an uncompromising war against Catholics which was fought on political, social and religious fronts. For the whole of the nineteenth century, and for a good part of the twentieth, the city of Liverpool became a real battlefield for the Protestant and Catholic groups. The battle was not a purely religious one. It was fought ostensibly on religious and ideological grounds, but the ideologies had a direct bearing on the economic and political problems and an immediate relevance to the tribulations of everyday life.

Against all this social deprivation and hardship the Roman Catholics had only one comfort, namely, their religion. It was through their religion that they suffered and survived, and in that sense Roman Catholicism was their hope in heaven and here on earth. For a long period of time the Roman Catholic clergy became the leaders of the Roman Catholic community at all levels of social existence and it is for this reason that they have always enjoyed an extra-special respect in Liverpool. For the Roman Catholic community, religion was always the most important factor of solidarity and a rich source from which its members drew immense strength. The authority of the church, the dogmas and all the practices which went with them were fully acknowledged by the Roman Catholic adherents because they were so very meaningful to their immediate life and social experience. The authority of the church was fully accepted as of divine origin, therefore there could be no internal conflict between that authority and the private lives, beliefs and experiences of the adherents.

Through the church, with its schemes for education and with the sense of belonging which it provided for them, Roman Catholics became gradually emancipated and took their share in the socio-economic life of the city. By the middle 1930s, they had achieved quite a good socio-economic status[6] compared with their condition during the nineteenth century.

During the last 30 or 40 years, the socio-economic structure of the Roman Catholic community in Liverpool has changed to the extent that one cannot speak any more in terms of social deprivation nor in terms of Irish immigrants.

These changes in the structure of the Roman Catholic community have their main basis, no doubt, in the wider socio-economic conditions of the city. It is equally beyond doubt, however, that through their religion, Roman Catholics made good use of social resources and opportunities. These changes, in turn, seem to have profoundly affected the loyalties of Roman Catholics to the doctrines and disciplines of their church.

### The present situation

It is common knowledge that Roman Catholics as a whole in Britain – and perhaps all over the world – have departed considerably from many traditional beliefs and practices of Roman Catholicism as it has been known in the past. As a result of this departure from the rigidity of traditional rules, a conflict has come about which is predominantly exemplified in the area of authority in the church.[7] During the present century, and especially during the last 20 years, there has developed, mainly through the laity, quite a new understanding of the concept of authority. This concept departs to a great extent from the juridical understanding of authority. In this new situation, instead of accepting authority as a set of rules and doctrines embodied in canon law, which is not to be questioned, fundamental emphasis is placed on human interpersonal relationships and on freedom of conscience.

This new emphasis on personal conscience as the arbiter of any external source of authority, including that of religion as propagated by the hierarchies of religious institutions, has had tremendous repercussions on the structure of authority in the Roman Catholic Church. Above all, this notion seems to be in conflict with any type of dictatorial or juridical understanding of authority in religion.

After Pope John's 'Aggiornamento' and especially after Vatican II, Roman Catholics seem to have become less and less convinced about the importance and/or the absolute authority of peripheral doctrines and disciplines of their church. The church's teachings on such things as purgatory and indulgences, for example, are not at present being given much attention because they do not affect the lives of the people directly. Doctrines with more immediate practical consequences such as birth control and the laws on divorce are directly raising conflict and opposition on the part of the laity because they affect them in their immediate lives.

Many Roman Catholics have reached the point of doubting such essential teachings of their church as those on papal infallibility (whatever interpretation may be given to it), confession and transubstantiation. This internal crisis is hardly surprising, since some changes have been kindled, at least indirectly, by the institution itself. In the documents of Vatican II, it is clear that most of the decrees of that council contain in themselves the arguments against the present structure of authority in the Roman Catholic Church. Article six of the decree on Ecumenism, for instance, reads

> Christ summons the Church, as she goes her pilgrim way, to that continual reformation of which she always has need, in so far as she is an institution of men here on Earth. Therefore, if the influence of events or if the times have led to deficiencies in conduct, in Church discipline or even in the formulation of doctrine (which must be carefully distinguished from the deposit itself of faith) these should be appropriately rectified at the proper moment.[8]

These changes and new dimensions in the theological and social thought of the church are now directly operative at the local level. They seem to be directly related to the general socio-cultural changes and tensions of all systems of values of our society. In Liverpool, they are directly reflected at the congregational level.

The old conflicts between Protestants and Catholics have almost completely disappeared and religious prejudice and intolerance have declined to a remarkable extent.[9] Instead, the weakening of religious ideologies and the ineffectiveness of traditional religious values in the present socio-cultural context has created a disparity between the authority of the church and the consciousness of the individual believer. In other words, it is at the point where the Roman Catholic ideology does not meet any longer the social, and indeed the religious consciousness of Catholics at the local level, that the conflict occurs. Some examples of this conflict, which is reflected at all levels of the church, will be given from the study of a Liverpool parish.

### The fieldwork

The Roman Catholic parish chosen for this study lies between two and three miles from the centre of the city of Liverpool. The area consists mostly of terraced housing and a large number of big houses which have been converted into flats since the war. A number of corporation flats have also been erected in the area recently. The district as a whole consists of a broad cross-section of population from the occupational and social status point of view. The records of the churches and the remarks of the clergy of the various denominations indicated that the population was fairly stable.

From the social stratification point of view, the majority of the inhabitants are working class with a good number of lower middle class and a few middle class householders.

The membership of the parish consists of 3,500 Roman Catholics. Of this population, about 50% are manual workers, about 30% to 35% are clerks of various kinds, shopkeepers, shop assistants and students. Another 15% are teachers, accountants, administrators, or have other professional occupations. Within the boundaries of the parish there are three Anglican churches, one Presbyterian, one Methodist, one Unitarian and one Quaker. There are quite a lot of ecumenical activities going on in the area and the Roman Catholic clergy and parishioners participate in many of these activities.

This parish is considered to be a flourishing one with a high level of church attendance. At least half the membership participates once a week in worship (mass),[10] a fact very significant for our discussion later. In general, this parish is a very active unit and there are four parish priests attached to it. They all seem to be fully occupied. The research was carried out over three years by means of participant observation. During this time, the investigator had the opportunity to come into contact with most of the practising members and had detailed and long discussions with them on the subject matter here discussed. The attendance at all kinds at services by the investigator, and his participation in the various activities, functions and parochial meetings proved most illuminating. Apart from gaining insight and a better understanding of the community, the participant observation enabled the investigator to gain a high degree of understanding of the actual personal beliefs of the adherents. On the basis of this close personal contact with the respondents, the investigator had many times to revise his conclusions as he kept gaining new insight and improved understanding of their personal beliefs.

Besides participating and observing generally, the investigator questioned a sample drawn from a sampling frame in which the criterion of eligibility was that the respondent should attend at least once a month one of the main occasions of worship and should be over 20 years of age. This age boundary was adopted and justified on the grounds that people over 20 years of age are capable of discussing their religious convictions at some depth.

No practising parishioners were excluded in principle since the investigation was designed to cover religious beliefs and practices of committed believers.

The priests were extremely helpful and gave the investigator all the assistance he needed. They carefully examined the list and indicated all the members under 20 years of age and all those who were not sufficiently active for the purpose of the study. The final list came to 1,180 members, from which a sample of 30 was drawn.

Fourteen members in the sample belonged to the age group 20–40 and 16 were over 40. This division into two age groups enabled the investigator to test the hypothesis that the younger members of the group – that is, those who were brought up and educated after the war – were less committed to the traditional doctrines of their church than those with a pre-war education and upbringing.

### Conflicts in the area of doctrine and discipline

Within the Roman Catholic tradition, most pronouncements of the Pope and the hierarchy always tended to be understood by the laity as authoritative statements of interpretation of divine truth. Although in the teaching of the Roman Catholic Church a distinction is made between statements of doctrine, which are infallible, and matters of discipline, which may vary from time to time and from place to place, in practice this distinction does not operate.[11]

Roman Catholic laymen today seem to be weary of all these theological elaborations which they find of little or no importance to their religious and social lives. This the respondents tried to express in almost every discussion with the investigator. In fact they were not interested in discussing the distinction between infallible doctrines and matters of discipline since most of them said such a distinction was meaningless. The discussion on doctrine and belief was introduced by general questions followed by more specific ones touching on special items of the teaching of the church.

The main general questions in this section were: Is there anything in the teaching of your church which you find difficult to accept? Would you be prepared to accept changes in the teaching of your church? What are the main points in the teaching of your church which you would like to see changed? These general questions elicited long discussions on individual doctrines which invariably impinged on the theme on authority in the church.

Twenty-two out of the 30 respondents in the sample stated that not only did they find it difficult to accept the whole teaching and authority of their church, but also that they disagreed radically at certain points with it. Thirteen of these disagreeing respondents were of the age group 20–40. Only one member of this group accepted the church's authority and teaching without questioning any part of it.

From the over-forties group seven respondents said that they accepted the authority of the church without reservations. The reasons they gave were summarized in the following statement by a 60-year-old male respondent: 'We can't question these things. You see, for us the Pope says something to the bishops, then the bishops to the priests, then the priests to us. It works that way. We, the Catholics, have no right to question what the Holy Father says. On these matters we just accept what we are told.' This section of respondents accepted all the changes introduced by Vatican II, and all the church's subsequent attempts to renew herself and make her teaching meaningful to contemporary man. There were some members, however, who were opposed to all the changes introduced by the church herself. These people were attached to the old traditions with great zeal and were strictly conservative. They thought that the church was giving in to the pressures of the secular world and that she had started 'compromising with the heretics'. This intransigent attitude seems to be represented by the extreme right wing of the Roman Catholic Church. From the interviews and from the study in general, however, it emerged that this attitude was held by a very small minority.

Those at this extreme end of the Roman Catholic Church seem to be at odds with the authority of the institution, not because it is conservative but because it compromises more than it ought to. In fact they regard the recent and present changes as being too far on the liberal side. The two respondents mentioned said, more or less, that the departure from a strict tradition is a slackening of the Catholic religion and a betrayal of the faith by the liberal laity and clergy who advocate these ideas.

This section of the Roman Catholic Church have on the whole passed middle age and they appear to stick stubbornly to traditional religious values, mainly because they are afraid of facing confusion in their convictions.

They are not prepared to abandon the security which their closed traditional system of beliefs has provided for them. Such a system of religious values has always provided these adherents with the 'totality of the truth'. Their religious values, in other words, represent a religious ideology embodying in itself a claim to infallibility which provides ready-made explanations of the world and the nature and destiny of man.

Abolition of this system is, therefore, a direct threat to the psychological and ideological security of those who adhere to it.

A similar attitude, one must say, is a characteristic to be found in many adherents of other religious ideologies, and has only been made to look intransigent by the cross-fertilization of various cultural values and ideas.

Speculating on this point, one could imagine that as the Roman Catholic Church is now rapidly changing and as a result of the changes which the wider society is undergoing, these people will find themselves more and more alienated from the institutional life of the church. As time goes on the wider socio-cultural system of values will satisfy their ideological needs less and less.

This aspect of conflict, nevertheless, seems to be one of the most insignificant ones which the Roman Catholic Church is facing at present. It has been already mentioned that people with such conservative beliefs are a small minority in the Roman Catholic Church, and their ideas and beliefs do not correspond sufficiently with the wider social reality to create a cohesive enough group within the church.

One should also mention that these ideological patterns have risen from, and belong to, socio-cultural situations of the past when they were operative and meaningful. The present socio-cultural structure of this society would hardly be appropriate for the operation of strict traditional ideas which have already been superseded.

A striking feature, which persisted throughout the investigation, was the anxiety of the respondents to show that their opposition or indifference towards certain teachings in no way meant that they were abandoning the faith or the church. It was also obvious throughout the survey that the whole problem seemed to be a conflict between personal beliefs and the institutional structure through which faith is mediated. The discussion on individual doctrines and practices indicated this area of conflict very clearly.

One of the most important doctrines within the Roman Catholic tradition, for example, is that of papal infallibility. The Pope as the Vicar of Christ on earth is the ultimate final arbiter and the final authority of any matter concerning the Roman Catholic Church.[12] Twelve respondents from the sample expressed open disagreement with this type of authority and grave doubts about the doctrine itself. Some, especially the younger, went so far as to criticize papal authority very severely. A young university graduate, for example, put his criticisms in the following way: 'The Pope claims infallibility, ultimate authority and monopoly of truth. To any thinking person this claim must be unacceptable. Infallibility is claimed only when he speaks *ex cathedra* and on matters of faith and morals only, but ultimately anything in the church can be a matter of faith and morals. I know that most Roman Catholics would not agree with what I say; in any case I am convinced that this attitude does not exclude me from being a Catholic and this is why I practise my faith in the church.'

The same kind of meaning was inherent in the protests of all the others who could not reconcile papal authority and infallibility with the dictates of their conscience. On doctrines such as the divinity of Christ and the Trinity, some respondents said that they found them incomprehensible but no one expressed disbelief or found them incompatible with everyday social experience. There was very little disagreement with the official teaching of the church on the sacraments. In fact nearly all respondents declared that they considered participation in the sacraments essential to being a Christian. It was obvious at the same time that most of them did not understand the theological implications of the church's teaching on these matters. On the whole it seemed that the symbolism of the sacraments was very remote from the reality and meaning of their lives.

Real disagreements and objections were brought out against one aspect or other of the teachings on matrimony and priesthood. The objections were not so much against their sacramental character but against specific aspects of these doctrines which the faithful found incompatible with the demands of contemporary life. The main point of disagreement on matrimony was the church's attitude on mixed marriages and divorce.

Again, on the sacrament of priesthood, no doubts were expressed about its validity, but many criticisms were made against aspects of priesthood such as celibacy, and the authoritarian elements inherent in its hierarchical structure. A young grammar school teacher was astonished at the certitude with which the clergy have assumed that the people should obey them. She put her opinions strongly: 'You see, people start thinking now that their conscience matters a lot. Obviously this was not so in our church even ten years ago. Some priests find it difficult to face up to the situation. They still think that they can tell you what to do even on matters in which the decision should be entirely your own.'

This kind of attitude was reflected in the opinions of three-quarters of the respondents and the general population of the parish. This was not in any sense a personal or anticlerical feeling. They were attacking an aspect of authority inherent in the priest's office which they found was contradictory to everyday experience, therefore difficult to understand and accept.

The changing attitude towards the traditional authority of the priesthood is very significant because it represents a different understanding of the concept of authority in the structure of institutional Roman Catholicism as a whole. In the present case the changing attitude towards the authority of priests is particularly important because in Liverpool especially the clergy stand very highly in the opinion of Catholics.

All the respondents were fond of their priests but the personal beliefs of the majority were in conflict with the traditional submissiveness to the authority of the priests.[13] Another area of acute conflict between the teaching of the church and the adherents' own attitude to it involved the various rules affecting some aspects of personal life.

A conspicuous example was the birth control issue. Most respondents showed great anxiety on this matter. Twenty of them spoke, without reservation, against what they called 'an unrealistic attitude of the church'. The people with these objections were mainly those affected directly by the church's teaching on this subject. Although there were some old couples and some old unmarried people who frowned at this rule it was mainly the young couples who were really torn between loyalty to the church and responsibility to life.

On the whole it seems that on this and other similar issues the faithful made up their own minds, ignoring the 'guidance' of the church. Furthermore, the respondents of the present study were convinced that this way of solving problems was not excluding them from the church but on the contrary it was good for the church herself. As a young clerk put his views: 'The Church needs reform from inside. It is no good abandoning the church because you disagree with it.' Then he added: 'I have had plenty of disagreements with my church's teaching, not only on birth control but even on more serious matters, but I think I have solved my difficulties without being unfaithful.'

The problem, however, seems to be more complicated than a simple personal decision, either to accept or to reject a church rule. In certain cases such as divorce and mixed marriages, for example, the individuals seem to feel helpless against the institutional authority of the church.

On this question again the respondents expressed their views at length. The younger people especially were very critical of the stance of the church in these matters. They were very anxious to point out that such rules were obsolete, as far as they were concerned, and the sooner there was a reform the better.

From what has been said it becomes obvious that the authority of the traditional teaching of the church has been seriously shaken in the minds of its members. The changes which the wider society has undergone, particularly in recent decades, and the watering down of traditional ideological structures, have made these values look meaningless, especially in the eyes of the younger generation.

### Conflicts in the area of worship and ritual

The essence of religious experience is inherent in communal worship.[14] In this sense worship is a symbolic action through which the worshippers experience the reality of their religion. In T. O'Dea's words: 'Religious rites are not performed primarily to achieve something but to express an attitude.'[15] Among the Christian churches the Roman Catholic Church is notable for her emphasis on worship and for the richness of symbolism used to express it.

Liturgical practice, otherwise known as the mass, has always occupied the very centre of Roman Catholicism. Even though Roman Catholics are obliged by Canon Law[16] to attend mass on Sundays and on special 'days of obligation', they are deeply attached to their worship. Evidence for this in Liverpool is the high attendance, the enthusiasm and the concern which the respondents showed on matters of worship. Most of them attributed crucial importance to mass, an attitude expressed in the typical remark: 'For us Catholics, mass is everything.' It was obvious that the ritual of the mass appealed to the majority and most of them found that participation in worship was a genuine religious act. The more educated respondents showed rather anxious feelings about the meaningfulness of worship. A young teacher put it like this: 'Although I believe that there is a kind of essential reality in worship, one gets the feeling that the whole performance of ritual in our church is out of date and does not reflect the truth which it is supposed to convey.' The meaning embodied in this view was also expressed in the answers of a good 50% of the respondents who felt that 'mass was important' but 'dry' and at times 'boring'. Most of the faithful seemed to have welcomed the changes introduced in Roman Catholic worship after Vatican II. Yet the great majority seemed to feel that the whole question of the renewal of worship was much more fundamental than a few changes here and there. It was obvious, from the way they spoke about worship, that liturgy is detached from their lives and most of the ritual performed within the church is somewhat devoid of meaning. On this point most of them seemed to be saying that there was very little the church itself could do to restore meaning in ritual. In fact some implied criticisms were expressed against an intellectual element in the church who try to intellectualize worship and impose meaning in ritual by theological interpretations and reinterpretations.[17] The feelings of the laity at this point were that meaning in worship derives primarily from immediate experience and true participation in the act of ritual. Meaningful ritual is a symbolic expression of life's essential meaning and as such directly relates to social reality and experience. According to the recent Vatican Council the Roman Catholic hierarchy seems to be fully aware of this and also aware of the fact that there is a gap now between Roman Catholic liturgy and life. The *Constitution on Liturgy*, article 21, for example, reads:

> In order that the Christian people may more securely derive an abundance of graces from the sacred liturgy, holy Mother Church desires to undertake with

great care a general restoration of the liturgy itself. . . . In this restoration both texts and rites should be drawn up so that they express clearly the holy things which they signify. Christian people, as far as possible, should be able to understand them with ease and to take part in them fully, actively and as befits a community.[18]

The implicit assumption in this statement seems to be that meaning in worship can be restored by theological analysis and renewal of old traditional patterns of ritual which fit with the Roman Catholic theological system. Although this is a fundamental step for renewal one wonders whether the structure of authority in the Roman Catholic Church would allow this renewal to take place at the grass roots of the institution, that is among the laity.

The structure of authority, being of a monarchical and dictatorial type, could hardly allow the emergence of renewal from below. The complaints of the respondents of this study about the church's imposing rules on attendance was an indication of this conflict.

Another fundamental factor which would make this kind of renewal extremely difficult is the fact that the Roman Catholic ideology itself would lose its own essential character if it were to allow such a high degree of participation by the laity. It would be too high a price for the institution to pay.

### Conclusions

From what has been said it can be easily inferred that in the Roman Catholic Church the type of authority which has previously derived its content and strength from a Tridentine and post-Tridentine theology is seriously shaken and can no longer be fully operative. This type of authority was functional when and where social and ideological conditions fostered it. In contemporary western society, however, where these ideological conditions have ceased to exist,[19] this type of authority is in conflict with the personal beliefs of the laity. In certain areas, especially where authority affects the personal lives of the adherents the conflict is acute. In other areas, where the laity can afford it, they make up their own minds and ignore the precepts of authority. These conflicts are exemplified to a very large extent in the beliefs and the conduct of the younger generation. The older element of the Roman Catholic Church seems to conform more to the traditional values of the institution.

It is not in any way clear what type of authority could replace the old one, but a more democratic type and a less centralized structure than the present one might fit better with the values of the wider society.

Officially, the Roman Catholic Church is continually introducing changes, but these changes are not in any sense pioneering. They are mainly brought about to accommodate the social pressures which have risen in our modern urban and industrial societies. All the same, tolerance on the part of the members and hierarchies of various religious bodies and the accommodation of broad inter-cultural values are carrying with them the tools which help to demolish the narrow structures of traditional Roman Catholicism.

It seems, nevertheless, that the peak of the crisis is yet to come. As our culture and our society attain a more and more universalistic character, and individuals reach a greater awareness of their individuality and freedom of conscience, these traditional structures will appear more and more unrelated to the lives and direct social experiences of Roman Catholic laity.

### NOTES

1. J. Banks discusses this point in *Readings in the Sociology of Religion*, ed. J. Brothers, Pergamon Press 1967, pp. 61–8. It is only in the last five years or so that sociologists in Britain have touched on this question, mainly through their studies on secularization. See Bryan R. Wilson, *Religion in Secular Society*, Watts & Co. 1966 and Penguin 1969; David Martin, *The Religious and the Secular*, Routledge & Kegan Paul 1969; R. Robertson, *The Sociological Interpretation of Religion*, Blackwells 1970; and the works by P. Berger and T. Luckmann.

2. To both Weber and Durkheim the question of authority in religion was of paramount sociological importance.

3. See F. Houtart, 'Conflicts of Authority in the Roman Catholic Church', *Social Compass*, XVI/3 1969, pp. 309–25. Also Jacques Leclercq, *La Liberté D'Opinions et Les Catholiques*, Les Editions du Cerf, Paris 1969.

4. The content of this essay is part of a larger empirical study conducted by the author in Liverpool for a Ph.D. Thesis. The title is *The Impact of Ecumenism on Denominationalism*, Ph.D. Thesis, Liverpool University 1969.

5. According to T. Burke, 296,231 Irish immigrants came to Liverpool in 1847 alone. 'They were all apparently paupers.' *Catholic History of Liverpool*, Liverpool 1910, p. 84.

6. Even then the Roman Catholics were quite low in the scale of social stratification compared with the Church of England and the Free Churches. According to the *Survey of Merseyside* (Hodder & Stoughton 1934, p. 337) 83·8% of the Catholic population were manual workers compared with 49·7% Church of England and 47·7% Free Church respectively.

7. F. Houtart, loc. cit.

8. *The Documents of Vatican II*, ed. W. M. Abbot, London-Dublin 1966, p. 350. The commentary on the documents observes at this point that 'it is remarkable, indeed, for an Ecumenical Council to admit the possible deficiency of previous doctrinal formulations.'

9. Only during the last two years, with the events in Northern Ireland, do the old prejudices seem to have been slightly stirred, but there is no real problem. The ideological and socio-economic problems of Northern Ireland seem to be sufficiently remote to cause no real conflict between Protestants and Catholics in Liverpool.

10. This was confirmed by the investigator himself.

11. There is an implicit inconsistency in this distinction, especially after the promulgation of the doctrine of papal infallibility by Vatican I. In actual fact the promulgation of this doctrine confirms the monarchical structure of authority in the Roman Catholic Church as exercised by the person of the Roman Pontiff. A comparison of the two following passages makes this inconsistency somewhat clearer.

Article No. 4 on the Decree in Ecumenism by Vatican II reads: 'While preserving unity in essentials, let all members of the Church, according to the office entrusted to each, preserve a proper freedom in the various forms of spiritual life and discipline, in the variety of liturgical rites, and even in the theological elaborations of revealed truth. In all things let charity be exercised' (*The Documents of Vatican II*, p. 349).

The principle of authority implied in this statement seems to be negated by the following passage from Pope Paul's Encyclical *Humanae Vitae* on birth control. Paragraph 6 reads: 'The conclusions at which the commission arrived could not, nevertheless, be considered by us as definite, nor dispense us from personal examination of this serious question; and this also because within the commission itself, no full concordance of judgments concerning the moral norms to be proposed had been reached, and above all, because certain criteria of solutions had emerged which departed from the moral teaching on marriage, proposed with constant firmness by the teaching authority of the Church. Therefore, having attentively sifted the documentation laid before us, after mature reflection and assiduous prayer, we now intend, by virtue of the mandate entrusted to us by Christ, to give our reply to these grave questions.'

12. Concerning the infallible authority and power of the Pope see *Codex Jurio Canonici*, Vatican City 1947 (Canons 1323 par. 2, 208, 1435, 1557, 1558, 1569, 19597).

13. The relations between clergy and laity in Liverpool have been discussed by K. Ward, *Priests and People*, Liverpool University Press 1965, pp. 54–64; and also by J. Brothers, *Church and School*, Liverpool University Press 1964, p. 87, where she says that 'the transformation of the social structure of Catholicism in Liverpool calls for the development of a new relationship between clergy and laity'.

14. E. Durkheim, *Elementary Forms of the Religious Life*, Allen & Unwin, 6th imp. 1968, especially the introduction.

15. *The Sociology of Religion*, Prentice Hall 1966, p. 20.

16. For the obligations of the Roman Catholic laity in worship, sacraments and sacramentals see *Canon Juris Canonici*, Vatican City (Canons 960, 1250, 1323 par. 1, 1324, 1325 par. 1).

17. On the questions of ritual and symbolism, see M. Douglas, *Natural Symbols*, The Cresset Press 1970, especially chs. 1–3.

18. *The Documents of Vatican II*, p. 146.

19. Northern Ireland is a notable exception. See the recent survey *Religion in Britain and Northern Ireland*, Independent Television Authority 1970.

# 3 The Religious Variable: Dependent, Independent or Interdependent?

*Kevin Clements*

CURRENTLY, many writers in the sociology of religion emphasize the basically dependent nature of the religious variable in the processes of social, economic and political change. They assert either that the religious institution is by its very nature incapable of exerting an independent influence on such types of change or, alternatively, that any possible religious influence is likely to be marginal and implicitly less important than the real determinants such as economic rationalization, urbanization and the political manipulation of scarce resources. Most of these theorists argue that the best any religious institution can do is to legitimate the *status quo* after the really significant changes have occurred. This theoretical emphasis in the sociology of religion is strongly weighted towards viewing the religious institution as adaptive and dependent and therefore fairly impotent in the face of more powerful economic, social and political realities.[1]

This paper, based on some aspects of religion in New Zealand, is an attempt to redress the emphasis by viewing religion as an independent variable capable of exerting considerable social and political influence on the processes of change. It would be unprofitable to survey the many arguments for and against this view as there are many notable antecedents for both positions.[2] Nor do I think it is particularly helpful to strike some *via media* by interpreting religion both as a dependent and an independent variable. Although this compromise view is attractive in that it seems to do greater justice to religious and social reality than a view which emphasizes dependence or independence, it can also lead to a lack of conceptual clarity and a consequent inability to explain or assess adequately the significance of religious institutions *qua* institutions. It also makes difficult the study of religious institutions in relation to wider social processes such as conflict, change, stability and control.

For the purposes of discussion, it will be assumed that religion is an independent variable capable of exerting a definite influence on a wide range of social action. Analysis of the role of religion in a period of social change offers interesting possibilities, since most writers investigating secularization identify periods of radical social, economic and political change as crucial for the initiation of the secularization process. Berger presents a minor modification of this view and claims an independent influence for religion at the beginning of the secularization process, but he goes on from this to state that religious symbolism and meaning are very rapidly superseded by other more significant factors after the initial changes have been legitimated. Nevertheless, Berger's analysis[3] goes part of the way towards eradicating a too materialistic or too idealistic view of religion.[4] Even Berger, however, fails to explain adequately the continuing independent influence of religion except in relation to privatized religion.[5] One is thus left with the impression that the religious institution is capable of exerting an independent influence on a macro-sociological level only when other institutions allow it to do so, either through their own failure to solve systemic problems or because they need a more general legitimation for particular courses of action. This latter view, although undoubtedly true in many respects, still assumes an initial religious dependence on non-religious institutions and non-religious processes.

A recently completed piece of research on the relation between religious and economic factors seems to throw light on this theoretical issue.[6] My study of social change in New Zealand during the depression suggests that there are very good grounds for interpreting religion as an independent variable. Since I was concerned with a period of radical social, economic and political change, some of the problems are thrown into clear relief.

A historical case study was made of the period 1929–38 in order to ascertain the nature and significance of religious ideology for the wider society and for the religious institutions themselves. Space does not permit a detailed account and attention will be focused on the general symbolism which religious opinion leaders developed in order to provide meaning in an otherwise meaningless environment, together with alternative ways of managing the economic situation other than the retrenchment policies which the Coalition Government advocated at the time.

What follows is a discussion about the ways in which the clerical and lay religious opinion leaders sought to redefine the social situation in such a way as to guarantee the restoration of meaningful social reality. Because the opinon leaders in any institutional sector are an active minority it is very difficult to generalize about the organizational acceptance or rejection of particular points of view. What evidence there is suggests that radical and often unpopular religious social teaching is accepted by a relatively small proportion of total church membership. But this does not detract from the fact that even unrepresentative opinion is capable of providing meaning and content for individuals both inside and outside the institution, and that if we are to make sense of any sort of religious expression, careful attempts must be made to assess the significance of such expression for the activities of the group.

The active minority of religious opinion leaders endeavours to:

(*a*) interpret and translate ultimate reality and transmit these insights to the brethren as well as to the society at large;

(*b*) safeguard and maintain religious interests and traditions and the particular theological ethos of their denomination; and

(*c*) struggle for relevance, both symbolically and actually in the ongoing process of reconciling the ideal and the actual.

In trying to do these things, opinion leaders produce symbolic systems that attempt to provide overarching religious meaning for committed members as well as for the wider society.

This is often a source of criticism of religious institutions, and the reason is fairly obvious. Frequently, people within the wider society make demands of the religious sector for which it is completely unequipped and for which very few other institutions are equipped. For example, it is unrealistic to expect specific economic or technical expertise from the religious institution, and yet many critics of religion criticize religious institutions for their lack of such expertise. However, although the religious institution often lacks the skills necessary to make sophisticated statements about a whole range of contemporary problems, this lack of skill does not necessarily mean that the religious institutional sector is being driven into an ever-diminishing circle of influence. On the contrary, it is at this crucial point that the independent influence of the religious institution is most obvious. Although the denominational and sectarian groups spend most of their time engaged in instrumental activities such as worship, social service, pastoralia and the creation of groups it can be argued that their primary role and the role which makes them distinctively religious is that of symbolic expression at the generalized level of values and norms.

In an urbanized and highly differentiated society the one thing that the religious institution can itself offer is a credible and valid meaning to the multiplicity of conflicting forces and processes that afflict modern societies. The need for such meaning is further emphasized by the fact that other institutional areas, such as education and the mass media, are failing to provide it.

There are a great many methodological dangers in historical parallels, but during the depression of 1929–35 there were many points of similarity with the present situation. The western world was confronted by intransigent economic crises, which in turn precipitated a number of political crises. The phenomenon of large scale unemployment created unprecedented structural fissures, a generalized breakdown in morale and in many cases a loss of national and individual identity. Such was certainly the situation in New Zealand.

Because social processes are made clearer under conditions of strain[7] the depression provides a good opportunity for investigating the significance of religious symbolism and ideology for the processes of change. At first sight, a Marxist analysis of the depression and of the role of the religious institutions as reflectors of the underlying economic reality seems to explain everything that happened. But although the Marxist analysis provides a very good explanation of the causes of the depression and some of the consequent strains, it fails to explain the significance of ideological factors for the processes of change.

During the depression religious social teaching in New Zealand and also in England[8] passed through three distinct stages. At each stage the opinion leader's understanding of the situation was significant in the sense that it was listened to, given wide coverage by the mass media and was frequently used by those holding and aspiring to political power. This meant that religious ideology had a salience that made it capable of exerting quite considerable influence on the development of symbolic systems that both supported the *status quo* and initiated change.

The first identifiable period, from 1929–31, was one of tacit and at times explicit support for the *status quo*. Religious leaders in all denominations – with some notable individual exceptions – advocated what may be called a puritan-pietist church-centred response to social and economic strain. There was an unwillingness on the part of the major religious denominations to make social and economic pronouncements because they, like the rest of the community, had no real understanding of what was happening and of possible ways of dealing with it. Thus the socio-religious ideologies of all denominations were in favour of stability and of supporting the Government at a time of national crisis. Such privatized concerns as personal morality, the importance of church attendance and the development of moral character were very much to the fore at this time. The Marxist critique of religious ideology as epiphenomenal would appear valid for this phase except that by supporting the *status quo* the religious opinion leaders were making almost identical statements to trade unionists and leaders of the unemployed, all of whom were equally bewildered by what was happening. During this time the churches responded in an instinctively religious way by agreeing to hold national days of prayer for the unemployed.

These national days of prayer were exploited by the Government and initially used to legitimate retrenchment and the development of labour camps in underdeveloped rural areas. The major denominations, Anglican, Presbyterian, Methodist and Roman Catholic, knew of no other ways of coping with the depression and for the first two years aquiesced, explicitly and tacitly, in whatever action the Government considered necessary. The Coalition Conservative Government readily exploited this willingness and asked the various churches to pray for national social and political unity to meet the national crisis. This was a rather shrewd political move because it meant that the opposition Labour party could then be classified as unpatriotic and unco-operative if it criticized or queried particular social or economic policies. The churches, like the majority of the community, readily co-operated with the Government as they felt sure that 'by tightening the belt for a little while longer the worst of the depression will pass and prosperity will rapidly return'.[9] This initial period of bewilderment and support for the *status quo* lasted until the end of 1931.

The second stage became apparent towards the end of 1931 and spanned the period 1931–4. Within this time a number of crucial changes occurred in the churches' development of social teaching and in the wider processes of social change. The Methodist and Roman Catholic churches – because of their slightly greater contact with those hardest hit by retrenchment – started developing social teaching that stood in radical contrast to earlier statements sympathetic to the maintenance of the *status quo*.

Roman Catholic opinion leaders endeavoured to relate the papal encyclical *Quadragessimo Anno* to the New Zealand conditions and in doing so they gradually articulated a systematic critique of Conservative monetary and social policies. Methodist opinion leaders, on the other hand, examined the practical implications of the Sermon on the Mount and evolved a form of Christian Socialism which they endeavoured to relate to the social and economic conditions.

These denominational ideological movements meant that when unemployment reached an all-time high towards the end of 1931, and deep structural rifts began to appear within the whole social system, the active minority of radical spokesmen within these churches had already begun defining the situation in a way that made sense to themselves and (hopefully) to other people as well. Both the Roman Catholic and Methodist Churches, by the beginning of 1932, had therefore acquired generalized beliefs about the situation that were acceptable to themselves and (as far as can be ascertained) to many other people. These beliefs were never seriously questioned or rejected within the particular churches. This meant that these two denominations, and to a lesser extent the Presbyterians and Anglicans, had developed general symbolic positions from which to view the specific events of the time.

These generalized sets of symbols were unable to exert very much influence on detailed thinking and policy-making because they lacked specificity. Thus they existed and had social reality as generalized feelings about the situation. However, specification occurred rapidly as soon as it became apparent to the churches' spokesmen that Governmental measures were not solving the economic crisis in a just and equitable manner.

The period 1931-4 was a period of religious and public dissatisfaction with Government policies. The existing ideologies of the Roman Catholic and Methodist Churches meant that these two religious groups responded very swiftly to particularly frustrating events, such as the Government decisions to withhold payment of relief money unless husbands and fathers left their homes and families to go and work in relief camps situated deep in the heart of New Zealand. It was at this time too that a significant minority of clergy in the Methodist Church and in the other denominations joined the Labour party. From the beginning of 1932 onwards it is possible to trace the increased expression of religious statements on political and economic affairs and the development of a slightly new religious emphasis in the Labour party's political rhetoric. In addition to these ideological effects of clerical involvement in the Labour party, the other important implication was that the radical clergy were able to develop a more specific understanding of the economic and political situation and of the ways and means of introducing change. In this way the generalized beliefs had by 1932 become more specific and politically sophisticated. Not only did the Labour party begin to employ religious rhetoric in publications and in debate, but the radical opinion-formers in all religious denominations began to employ socialist rhetoric in their interpretations of 'ultimacy'.

This tendency was accelerated and to a large extent precipitated by a series of violent riots in 1932, which helped crystallize the discontent that had been accumulating since 1930. Violence served to polarize the society into two groups, those sympathetic towards the rioters and what they stood for and who espoused radical change; and those who were unsympathetic towards the rioters and who preferred to let Adam Smith's invisible hand move in its own time. The Methodist and Roman Catholic Churches, while not condoning the violence, did align themselves with the former position and sympathized with the rioters and their cause. It was this and other similar support for groups endeavouring to alter the situation that provided the religious institution with legitimation to extend its social teaching and make further symbolic as well as instrumental contributions to the development of new social reality.

The change-oriented minority in each denomination certainly encountered some opposition for their zealous advocacy of economic and political change, and it is possible to identify opinion leaders in every denomination who emphasized values in favour of the *status quo* and the Conservative Government.[10] The presence of persons advocating support for the *status quo* did not, however, affect the extent to which the change-oriented ideologies of the activists gave considerable significance to those people who were working for change through the Labour and other intellectual movements such as economic and social research groups. The Labour party's ideology and the religious and social teaching that was developed from 1932–4 became increasingly hostile to the apparent indifference of the Coalition Government. Both the Labour party and the churches, in response to the unemployed and the wider Labour movement, developed detailed critiques of what was awry in Government policies. They also began to suggest and develop alternative schemes. These alternatives were often naive and impracticable but very gradually they gave rise to the idea of a Welfare State where the Government assumed responsibility for the care and maintenance of all its citizens irrespective of age, sex, race or physical condition. This idea emerged in response to the resolutions, plans and protests of the churches, the trade union movement, the Labour party and influential intellectuals sympathetic to the development of a corporate state. Each group had its particular contribution to make to the final conception and it was at this point that the independent variability of the religious institutions was made manifest. Because they lacked the economic expertise to make specific proposals about such things as public expenditure or internal loans, religious groups were forced to develop another role, that of a provider of generalized values and beliefs about the total situation both from an individual and corporate perspective.

The third definable period, therefore, is that from 1934 until December 1935 when the Labour party won a landslide victory at the polls. During this period religious opinion leaders developed new values or modified previously-held values which were favourable and positively encouraging to radical social and political change. Religious spokesmen developed a socio-political ideology which they saw as relevant to both the economic and social realities and to their understanding of the ultimate in the existing situation. They spent much time condemning the injustice of poverty and the Government mismanagement of the economy, and proposed many alternative positive measures by way of a solution. The Depression was a time of slogans; thus 'Poverty in the midst of plenty' was condemned as roundly by the churches as by the Douglas social credit and the Labour parties. All denominations initiated and supported a Crusade for Social Justice and many individuals advocated modified forms of Christian Marxism. But the major role that the churches played, which involved no other group but the Labour party in its rhetorical policy statements, was to provide generalized theological and moral values and beliefs about justice and injustice, about the ethics of poverty and the teaching of the church with regard to the poor and exploited; and most importantly, values which provided religious legitimation for the Labour party – which up until 1934 had been unable to establish its credentials as a legitimate non-communist party. The Labour party was identified by most religious opinion leaders as the truly Christian party, as the party which most adequately expressed Christianity in practice, and which came closest to translating into reality the religious values which the churches' spokesmen had been expounding over three years.

Thus the religious institutions endowed with specifically religious content a situation which had been devoid of meaningful economic and political content for a considerable period of time. They did so, not so much by espousing particular policies as other symbol makers did, but by expressing general values held to be valid for the New Zealand situation at the time and for all time. By the end of 1935 every major religious denomination, including the Presbyterian and Anglican as well as the Roman Catholic and Methodist, had advocated radical social and political change in order to initiate a new system where human values, and not cost-benefit analyses, would become the major criteria by which economic and political decisions would be made.

This undoubtedly helped to legitimate the Labour party's bid for power since there was a convergence between religious and political rhetoric on this point, and in the course of the election campaign great use was made of clergy in chairing Labour party meetings and speaking in support of Labour candidates. Ten clergymen stood for the Labour party and three were elected. After the Labour party had gained power, initiated changes and legitimated its existence instrumentally through social security legislation and the introduction of a planned economy, it did not have to rely so much on the supporters who had put it into power in the first place. Nevertheless, religious spokesmen positively legitimated the Welfare State after legislation was enacted and they also welcomed the other changes that the Labour party initiated in order to gain direct control over the whole situation.

### Conclusion

Space does not permit a more detailed analysis of the ways in which the churches' social teaching responded to cultural and structural stimuli, but enough has been said to demonstrate the points at which the religious spokesmen were able to exert an independent influence on the direction of change.

For the first period, there is little doubt that socio-religious ideology was almost completely dependent on non-religious definitions of the situation. This paralleled a wider inability to understand what was happening. In the second period, the religious variable acted interdependently, attempting to contribute towards a widespread analysis of what was happening and of appropriate attitudes and actions to take in the circumstances. The riots of 1932 helped focus and crystallize discontent and thereafter the religious institutions sought to develop an independent approach to the situation. This meant formulating generalized values and beliefs so that by the third period it is possible to say that the religious variable exerted considerable independent influence on social change, by legitimating the agents of change – the Labour party – and by suggesting specific innovations that the Labour party might adopt in order to bring about a specifically Christian solution to the problem. It was by producing religious symbols to interpret the situation that the religious institutions exerted an independent influence on the changes that occurred.

## NOTES

1. See for example C. Glock and R. Stark, *Religion and Society in Tension*, Rand McNally, Chicago 1968; also Bryan R. Wilson, *Religion in Secular Society*, Watts & Co. 1966 and Penguin 1969; and for a dissenting view David Martin, *The Religious and the Secular*, Routledge & Kegan Paul 1969.

2. R. W. Green, *Protestantism and Capitalism; The Weber thesis and its critics*, D. C. Heath and Co., Boston 1965, contains some useful statements of the general problem.

3. P. Berger, *The Social Reality of Religion*, Faber & Faber 1969.

4. Ibid., p. 127.

5. This point was made by Margaret Scotford Archer and Michalina Vaughan in their article 'Education, Secularization, Desecularization and Resecularization', *Sociological Yearbook of Religion in Britain 3*, SCM Press 1970, pp. 130–46.

6. K. P. Clements, *The Churches and Social Policy: A study in the relationship of ideology to action*. Unpublished Ph.D. Thesis, Victoria University of Wellington, New Zealand 1970.

7. N. J. Smelser, *Social Change in the Industrial Revolution*, Routledge & Kegan Paul 1959; and also *Theory of Collective Behaviour*, Routledge & Kegan Paul 1962.

8. J. Oliver, *The Church and Social Order*, Mowbrays 1968.

9. G. Forbes (PM of New Zealand 1930) in *The Evening Post*, Wellington, 6 February 1930.

10. For a more detailed discussion and elaboration of this point, see M. A. Neal, *Values and Interests in Social Change*, Prentice-Hall, New Jersey 1965.

# 4   The Anglo-Catholic Priest : Aspects of Role Conflict

*Francis Absalom*

THE Anglo-Catholic party has existed in the Church of England for 130 years. Emerging from Tractarianism in the 1840s and 1850s, it sought a return to standards of church authority, doctrine and worship which it saw as part of the church's heritage, though lost through centuries of Erastianism. The means it adopted in pursuit of these goals, particularly the attempts to establish catholic doctrines such as the Real Presence of Christ in the eucharist and the desirability of sacramental confession, and elaborately ritualistic services, as legitimate components of Anglican belief and worship, brought it sharply into conflict with the majority opinions of nineteenth-century Anglicanism. Throughout the years from 1850 onwards, though to a diminishing extent in recent decades, controversies over such issues were an ongoing part of Anglican church life; in the course of time, Anglo-Catholics achieved most of the goals for which they fought, and an initially deviant group became firmly institutionalized in the church, bringing about substantial changes in legitimate forms and beliefs in the process.[1]

Coincident with the emergence of Anglo-Catholicism from Tractarianism occurred the structural differentiation of the role of 'priest' from that of 'Anglican parson'. Changes in the nature of Anglo-Catholicism itself are apparent in the contrast between the 'traditional' version of this role, dominant in the period from about 1860–1945, and the 'new' version which has slowly emerged in the post-war years. The presentation of both roles here is in the form of ideal types in order to highlight their distinctive features – empirically there was considerable variance, and a range of permutations of role elements.

David Martin has drawn a characteristically succinct pen-portrait of the older type of Catholic priest, 'sartorially correct even down to the biretta and the kind of rimless glasses favoured by cardinals . . . combining the priestly turbulence which terrorises bishops with an unblinking assertion of ecclesiastical authority'.[2] The origins of this type can be traced back to the middle of the nineteenth century as recorded in the history of an ecclesiastical pressure group such as the Society of the Holy Cross (known as SSC from its Latin title *Societas Sanctae Crucis*). Founded in February 1855, the SSC sought to establish the Catholic movement upon firm foundations by creating an elite corps of clergy with clear goals, a strong system of personal discipline and a unity which would enable resistance to attacks upon them from outside.

> The chief end of SSC was to build up the priestly character. It dealt with such matters as early rising, Mass, prayer, self-examination, regular confession, intercession and retreat. It was aware that the church needed indeed able men – organisers, social, controversial – but beyond all, what she needed most was an order of men who cultivated the inner life – 'full of eyes within' – those who were 'set apart' (sanctified). And so the Society fostered the ecclesiastical spirit; not indeed the unreal, so often mistaken for it of a stiffness towards laymen and the things of the world, but the desire in the soul of the priest to live up to his vocation, not avoiding what interested laymen, but always bearing in mind the recollection of his priesthood and its eternal character'.[3]

SSC was never great in numbers, and at the present time may be taken as representative of the 'extreme' Papalist wing of Anglo-Catholicism, along with similar groups such as the Catholic League; a wing now very much in a minority. However, its influence in the nineteenth and early twentieth centuries as a focus of opposition to attempts to limit the Catholic advance, and its concentration upon the role of the priest as central to the success of the movement, give it a significance beyond its numbers. Among its leaders were Lowder, Mackonochie, Carter, Nihill, Ommanney, Baverstock and Reginald Kingdon, all famous as pioneers in the introduction of Catholic doctrine and ritual at the parish level, and a considerable number of prominent Catholic priests have been associated with it at some time.

The ideological elements in the self-definition of SSC members clearly formed a significant source of strength for the conflicts which arose in the second half of the nineteenth century, as Anglo-Catholicism spread from its original narrow, Oxford-centred base to penetrate parish life throughout the country. The priestly role was sharply defined: as a man under discipline, the representative of the divine at the local level, the priest saw himself as entrusted with a responsibility which he must defend against the opposition of rioting mobs, protestant hecklers, dissident laity and hostile or indifferent bishops. This responsibility was not directly to the Church of England as then constituted, but to a broader conception of catholicity which he saw as inherent in Anglicanism, if not always recognized.

> The English Provinces claimed to be both National and an integral part of the One Catholic Church of Christ. While the former claim gave them the limited liberty of a National Church, the latter claim bound them to the obedience due to the whole Church. The constitution, continuity, canons and Prayer Book of the English Church revealed this to be her mind. The bishops meant by the spirit, or mind, of the Church, their own minds and, in subjection to the State, seemed to think that by the 'greater price' of Erastian bonds, they had 'obtained the freedom' of ignoring Catholic claims. The obedience they asked for was a phantom one, which faded into thin air when measured by the standards of the Ordination Vows, or the Canonical Obedience which a priest has to render to his bishop. Obedience to their demands would have meant disobedience both to the Catholic Church and to the historical interpretation of the Prayer Book, and to the Church's true mind.[4]

Such a conception of the basis of their authority was not confined to SSC members only, but was part of the intellectual apparatus by which a much larger group of Catholic priests justified their position, and thus their *de facto* disobedience to *de jure* authority. It was expressed in similar terms by many, and also by the lay leaders of other Catholic organizations, such as Lord Halifax of the English Church Union (founded 1859);[5] and the extremism which such a view could engender was not in doubt in George Orwell's mind when he described Anglo-Catholicism as the ecclesiastical equivalent of Trotskyism.[6] On such a basis was founded the history of ritualist strife from the 1850s down to relatively recent times. The introduction of elaborate ceremonial and the apparatus of Catholic worship – vestments, servers, incense, statues, votive candles, auricular confession, observation of holy days not in the Prayer Book, and of ceremonial which had not been a part of Anglican worship for centuries – for example, the Holy Week services – involved a radical shift in the nature of the Anglican church which could only be brought about by a process of conflict and its gradual resolution. Undoubtedly this conflict was at its height in the period from 1860–1930. Catholic innovations provoked opposition from the Protestant faction in the Church of England, institutionally embodied in organizations such as the Church Association, which attempted to invoke legal sanctions against ritualist clergy in a series of cases before lay and ecclesiastical courts from the mid-1860s onwards; and which also sought to enable the church to define its norms so unambiguously that the 'interpretations' of the 'mind of the church' upon which Catholics founded their case could be decisively refuted. So far as the first aim of the Protestant attack was concerned, the high points were the passing of the Public Worship Regulation Act of 1874, the long-drawn-out prosecution of Mackonochie of St Albans, Holborn, from 1868–83, and the imprisonment for varying periods of five priests in the years 1877–87. The second aim found expression in the Ritual Commission of 1867, the Royal Commission on Ecclesiastical Discipline of 1904, and the Prayer Book controversies of the 1920s. It would be misleading to attribute such endeavours solely to Protestant agitation – in a large measure they also reflected the alarm of more moderate sections of laity, clergy and episcopate about the extent to which church order as they understood it was being destroyed. However, in the event, a succession of legal decisions legitimated many of the ritual innovations; legal sanctions proved both counter-productive, in that the disquiet aroused by the imprisonment of clergy far outweighed any satisfaction at the attempt to maintain discipline, and also vacuous, in that they were disregarded by many Catholic clergy. The nature of this failure is plainly revealed by the Report of the 1904 Commission, in the extent of ritualism described by witnesses and its distribution across the country. Similarly, the Protestant use of mob coercion and interruption of services created martyrs of the clergy thus persecuted while failing to intimidate them, and aroused as much disgust as sympathy for the Protestant cause among outsiders.[7]

The position of the bishops, and their relations to their turbulent priests, were varied and inconsistent. Broadly they concerned themselves with the maintenance of church order, but this had a changing interpretation as Catholic norms of worship and doctrine became progressively institutionalized through legal legitimation, clerical defiance and lay acceptance. In successive periods they opposed the famous 'Six Points' of ritual which formed the focus of conflict in the late nineteenth century; they fought a battle against incense in the years 1890–1920; and in the period after the First World War an attempt was made to restrict non-Prayer Book services connected with the doctrine of the Real Presence of Christ in the bread and wine of the Holy Communion. In all these cases the episcopal side lost – partly because of the ineffective sanctions which it could bring to bear, partly because of the sympathy felt by many bishops for the pastoral endeavours of the Catholic clergy. A number of bishops were profoundly influenced by Tractarian ideals (for example King of Lincoln, who was himself prosecuted for ritualism before the Archbishop of Canterbury's court in 1890), and many of the younger Tractarian leaders eventually became bishops;[8] though this did not necessarily lead them to favour 'extremism', at least they possessed diffuse affinities with the school of thought of which the extremists were members. (To qualify this point, however, it should be noted that accession to high office could bring about a measure of conservatism with the acceptance of wider responsibilities.[9]) To the extent that pastoral sympathy or the sharing of broader ideals influenced the episcopate, a united front against ritualism could not be presented, and Catholics gained ground. During the period in which Frederick Temple and A. F. Winnington-Ingram were bishops of London, for example, significant advances were made.[10] Temple liked Anglo-Catholics because they were workers, and gave them their head – the result was described as liturgical chaos. His successor, Mandell Creighton, attempted moderation, forbidding some of the Holy Week services and those such as Benediction, Rosary, Litany of the Saints, and services for the dead, which involved the Roman doctrine of purgatory; also he restricted the use of incense and reservation of the sacrament of Holy Communion – 'the vestments question had been settled by disobedience in the previous generation'.[11] Winnington-Ingram attempted to continue this policy, but it was during his long episcopate that Anglo-Catholicism became entrenched in the diocese. He was willing to permit a moderate Catholicism, and achieved some success through the exercise of personal influence upon clergy, but his instructions were never in writing and more often exceeded in practice, and in the case of a 'completely Romanized' church such as St Saviour's, Hoxton,[12] he could do little but place the parish under discipline and later appoint a slightly more moderate incumbent – to do this he had to wait for the death of the extremist Vicar. His refusal to attempt stronger sanctions attracted criticism from his fellow bishops, and presented problems for his successor.[13] Attempts by other bishops to get general acceptance of a prescribed limit to churchmanship, as by Bell of Chichester in the 1930s,[14] and attacks on the practice of Reservation, as by Barnes of Birmingham,[15] similarly achieved limited and short term success. The documentation of episcopal attempts at discipline and restraint is extensive and cannot be dealt with further here, but the present position would seem to be that within very broad limits, influenced largely by the extent of lay opposition in the parish, Anglo-Catholic clergy are permitted by bishops to follow their own inclinations.[16]

Relations with bishops were important to the priest in a sense other than that of overt conflict or support. It was the bishop who made a man priest through the rite of ordination. In this ceremony the priest believed he received the power to carry out sacramental functions, principally the celebration of 'the miracle of the mass' by which Christ is made present in the bread and wine of the Holy Communion. Yet the bishop who ordained him might have a quite different understanding of ordination, namely that it involved the commissioning of men to perform conventional clerical duties and not of priests to offer the sacrifice of the mass. This point might be explicitly stated by the bishop in his address to ordination candidates. Bishop and ordinand thus might take opposed views of the rite in which they were joint participants, and the future Catholic priest had to find some satisfactory explanation of the correctness of his own belief. This was done by contending that ordination is valid independent of the bishop's intention. A similar device was used to deal with the problem of how a non-Catholic Anglican minister could be said to celebrate a valid mass while believing it to be no more than a memorial meal and rejecting any doctrine of the Real Presence.

The traditional priest in his ideal-typical form was an authoritarian paternalist. At least three reasons for this can be advanced. Firstly, such an attitude was expected of the more general role of 'parson' in nineteenth and early twentieth-century England, as prescribed by culture and social structure, and the priest adopted this as part of his cultural baggage. Secondly, his understanding of the distinctive character of his role encouraged such a pattern of behaviour, as the earlier quotation from Embry suggests: he was a man set apart as sacramental agent of the divine, ordained to celebrate the Sacred Mysteries and to teach and lead his people. Thirdly, his structural location as the agent of a deviant religious subculture, innovating in parishes of low Catholicity, and maintaining or enhancing churchmanship in established Catholic parishes, placed upon him an additional responsibility, that of a leader in the vanguard of the movement for the conversion of England to 'the Faith of our Fathers'.

Such a self-image generated social distance in relations with parishioners, and this was enhanced by such role signs as the priestly biretta, cloak and cassock, worn for everyday duties around the parish, and the title of 'Father' which became common as a mode of addressing priests. Considerable status differences also existed between the overwhelmingly middle-class clergy and many of their lower status flock (though there was also a significant element of middle-class and affluent laity). Commitment to celibacy by a significant minority of priests also added to the distinctive character of the role, while at the same time bringing about certain psychological strains. Priests also attracted sometimes unwelcome attention from two of the stereotypical lay followers of the movement – ardent young men and lonely middle-aged ladies – and in such cases social distance could be an effective protection.

At the same time an undoubted charisma resulted from the priest's apartness, and from the social concern which many expressed. The early history of Anglo-Catholicism is studded with the names of heroes of the Faith – Lowder, Wainwright, Mackonochie, Dolling, Stanton and others – and with legends of their work among the poor in slum parishes. This charismatic element was also enhanced by the evident self-sacrifice which such men displayed, both in social action and in the abandonment of hope of career advancement. A number of priests went to Catholic parishes knowing that by their actions they might be committed to a lifetime as a curate in the same church, possibly under discipline from their own bishops (which meant that they were effectively cut off from diocesan life along with their parishioners), and prevented from officiating in other dioceses by episcopal inhibition.

Structural isolation of this sort had certain advantages. The priest was able, within the constraints set by parishioners' support and the visits of hostile Protestants, to develop parish and churchmanship as he chose. Since a number of clergy had private incomes which they were more than ready to devote to the furtherance of the Catholic cause, they were able to transform their churches into eclectic replicas of Continental Roman Catholicism, adorned with statues, candles, confessionals and tabernacles, and to ensure that the liturgy was performed with maximum elaboration and splendour. Where personal income was not available for this purpose, expenses might be met by affluent lay enthusiasts, or from the funds of religious pressure groups such as the Church Union, the Catholic League, the Confraternity of the Blessed Sacrament or the Guild of All Souls.

Another advantage derived from the physical isolation of parishes, either in the remote countryside, or in 'urban villages'. Here social life might be focused upon the church to a greater extent than in more accessible areas, since there were few alternative attractions, and forms of Catholic community could become established. In addition, in a few cases, funds were employed to buy houses and cottages for the use of Catholics drawn from further afield by the attraction of 'full Catholic privileges'. Thus a remote village church such as Throw-leigh in Devon could boast in the mid-1940s a daily mass attendance of 12; 9,000 church attendances and 5,000 communions a year; weekly Holy Hour and Benediction, and many penitents.[17] The dis-advantages of such isolation were firstly, the encouragement it gave to priestly individualism: church and parish were the property of one dominant figure who moulded them according to his own views, drawn selectively from the available apparatus of Catholicity, and sometimes eccentric; and secondly, the development of a parochialism which militated against the integration and cohesiveness of the move-ment as a whole.

The priest experienced difficulties in role maintenance from a num-ber of sources. Firstly, since for a large part of the period under consideration Anglo-Catholicism was in conflict with the dominant norms of the church, he might expect trouble with the bishops, non-Catholic clergy and hostile laity from outside the parish. Secondly, the movement to which he belonged itself possessed marked internal divisions. At one extreme the papalist groups sought corporate re-union of the Church of England with the Holy See, and followed Roman Catholic norms so far as they could both doctrinally and liturgically, to the extent that their churches were Roman in all but name. At the other extreme, the Prayer Book Catholics generally conformed to the Book of Common Prayer in their services, while adopting those practices which were legally permitted by Anglican authority. This latter group, while accepting the notion of Anglican-ism as part of the universal Catholic church (in itself a doctrine generally held by Anglicans of all parties), rejected the extreme view that this necessarily led to defiance of episcopal authority or to the adoption of Roman beliefs and practices. In between these two extremes, a variety of permutations, which it would be superfluous to describe here, existed. Similarly, in terms of attitudes to the world as expressed in social and political commitment, a variety of postures were held, from left wing affiliations and social involvement to con-servatism and a withdrawn sacramental pietism. Thus the movement was fragmented in various respects at an early stage; its ideology was diffuse and unified action was possible only to a limited extent.[18] This increased priestly isolation.

Thirdly, in his own parish, the priest might experience conflict with parishioners. This was not inevitable, and in established Catholic parishes it might be minimal or non-existent – though even here there was a thread of ongoing opposition to anything that smacked of 'Romanizing'. Practices coming within this category were extremely varied, and reflected parish conservatism rather than ideological opposition. Comments in the literature suggest that the Anglo-Catholic layman's devotion to 'what Father X did' was as strong as that of his evangelical or broad church counterpart to another kind of tradition.

In non-Catholic parishes, the priest saw his task as one of Catholicization. Though this did not necessarily lead to conflict, a measure of dissidence was common. The introduction of vestments might cause the loss of a substantial section of the congregation; attempts to alter the music from a staple diet of hymns and psalms to the rarefied delights of plainsong or a Byrd mass could decimate the choir; parish council elections could result in the priest being confronted with a united and hostile body of laity; and references in sermons to the Virgin Mary as 'Our Lady' or the communion service as 'mass' frequently provoked mutterings of 'high church nonsense' and 'popery', or even walk-outs. There were cases where a transition from conventional Anglicanism to Catholic extremes occurred without opposition, and even with general lay support, but these were rare; also in newly built churches a Catholic tradition might be established from the start; but the more usual pattern was of slow advance against varying degrees of opposition.

A fourth problem for role maintenance was the advance of secularization, especially after the First World War. Prior to this, even in the context of the widespread areligiosity shown by various surveys from the 1851 Religious Census onwards, many ritualistic churches attracted large congregations.[19] In the post-war period, while the Catholic movement as a whole gained support, individual parishes began to decline. Thus the increased support derived from an increase in the *number* of Catholic parishes, but seldom from growth *within* parishes. This is apparent in comments in journals of the day, and also in individual parish records, where a decline in gross numbers of communicants can be traced from the 1920s onwards. It is important to recognize that such a decline had begun so early (though of course it has been vastly accelerated since 1945) in order to understand the position of many parochial clergy in the last 50 years. A number of established parishes experienced declines which they only partly understood and could not arrest. Moreover, the younger clergy, entering parochial work often after an early period of intense Catholic socialization,[20] found themselves in a situation where triumphalism was brought up against the cold reality of indifference.

Finally, a continuing problem for Anglo-Catholic priests derived from the use by many of Roman Catholicism as a source of doctrinal and liturgical standards. At the same time, many expressed a defensive antipathy to the 'Romans', based upon their belief in the Church of England as 'the Catholic church in this land'. The Catholic ideology generated numerous paradoxes, but few more basic than the problem of authority. Catholics based themselves upon the authority of the church, yet they were continuously in conflict with their own ecclesiastical hierarchy; and Rome, the prime institutional locus of Catholic authority, denied their claims and rejected their orders as invalid.[21] Not surprisingly, some priests experienced profound self-doubt, leading to eventual conversion (or 'poping'); as one convert priest wrote:

> I went about for weeks in a state of uncertainty, undecided in my conscience as to whether I was morally bound to face things out or not – wretched under the suspicion that what 'Rome' said might be true – that I was no priest; that my 'mass' was no mass at all; that I was genuflecting before . . .? That my 'absolutions' were useless. The more I prayed about it, the more unreal my ministry appeared.[22]

To cope with this variety of challenges to role maintenance, a number of devices were available. The ideology might be dogmatically affirmed, or defended in constant argument, with elaborate source citation for controversial views. The priest's membership of Catholic societies gave him a sense of brotherhood with fellow Catholics in the struggle for the conversion of England, as did pilgrimages to Walsingham and other famous shrines; the journals of the societies, and papers such as the *Church Times* or the *Guardian*, with their reports of growing Catholic parishes elsewhere and fresh Episcopal or Protestant defeats, gave him an assurance of future triumph; and the performance of his sacerdotal functions – the daily mass, the hearing of confessions from his few penitents, the regular retreat with a religious order for spiritual recharging – reinforced his self-image as a man set apart for the work of God in the midst of the heathen. It is in this light that one can interpret in the parish records of churches, the daily mass, year after year, with only one or two communicants (the priest, his wife if he had one, perhaps an enthusiastic layman, or more probably a laywoman), and the commemoration of the feasts of Corpus Christi or the Sacred Heart, carefully recorded in red ink in the parish register. Here was the priest's justification: though he might have to guard his tongue in relations with most parishioners, and restrain his ritual; though in his parish there was little or no sign of the return to the Faith which his leaders predicted, yet still in his church was offered the daily sacrifice of the mass; his difficulties and failures were daily laid before God; and his indelible office of priest was confirmed. To such role signs (also displayed daily by the wearing of cassock and biretta, sometimes despite offensive comments),[23] he could cling, even in the face of such ultimate rejection as physical expulsion from his parish. Thus Sandys Wason, of Cury in Cornwall, driven out with all his belongings by a group of hostile farmers and unable to enter his church, nonetheless returned to a cottage in the village to perform his priestly duty:

> 'Must be there to say Mass for those stupid people,' he said. 'Can't do anything else for them.'[24]

By contrast with the traditional pattern, the main features of the priest's role today will now be briefly indicated. Firstly, he is part of a movement manifestly both in decline and undergoing radical change. The 1968 Church Union Congress was a pale shadow of the triumphant Anglo-Catholic congresses of pre-war years, although widely interpreted as effectively displaying the changed orientations of the movement. Congregations have fallen rapidly, and in some cases are virtually non-existent; in many places the daily mass is a thing of the past; remote country churches can be found where the Sunday sung mass attracts a congregation of half a dozen, the statues are dusty, the sanctuary lamps unpolished and unlit, and the tabernacle empty. A number of well-known churches were destroyed by wartime bombing and have not been rebuilt; and programmes of pastoral reorganization (interpreted by some as anti-Catholic in intention) have closed others. The Parish Communion has replaced High Mass in some places, with a subsequent decline in traditional churchmanship. Many of the Catholic societies have experienced a reduction in membership and complain about lack of support for their festivals and meetings – thus their influence on the priest's self-image is now in terms of association with moribund cultic forms rather than of connection with a thriving movement.

Two major priestly role types exemplify current problems of the Catholic party. Firstly, there is a continuing traditional type, small in numbers and carrying on an uphill struggle to maintain full ritual and doctrine. This group is under pressure, not only from the sources indicated above, but also from the generation gap which exists between them and the younger clergy who sometimes act as their curates. A clerical version of intergenerational conflict can arise in which a decline which is basically social structural in origin can be attributed for the purposes of argument either to a loss of Catholic fullness and discipline, or to the fruitless attempt to maintain old-fashioned ways. The older group is often plainly reluctant to acknowledge the extent of decline, and is critical of open discussion of facts and causes as the 'washing of dirty linen in public'.[25]

The second role type is that of the newer Catholic clergy, particularly those ordained since the 1950s. Priestly charisma and authoritarianism are no longer structurally available. Any possibility of building up traditional forms of authority or charismatic dominance is hampered by the comparatively high level of mobility, compared to previous periods, of both clergy and laity. Priests, especially curates, tend to move frequently, partly because of changing patterns of diocesan needs, partly in search of wider responsibilities, and possibly also because of a diminishing sense of commitment to one parish as a vocation for life. This contrasts sharply with the older pattern of long incumbencies, extreme examples of which may be found in the parish of Throwleigh, mentioned above, which has had only three Rectors in this century, Hinton Martel, in Dorset, which has had four, or Bridgerule, in Devon, where Frank Hawker Kingdon was vicar for 70 years; and a number of less striking examples could also be quoted. Similarly, increased mobility in the general population restricts the supply of laity available to perform church roles and to legitimate the priest's authority on the basis of tradition. For both these reasons, the older authoritarian paternalism is now rare.

The reduction of status differences consequent upon the recruitment of clergy from lower social strata than previously also brings priests closer to their laity. The biretta is seldom worn, and the cassock less frequently. Clerical attitudes to the decline of authority in the old sense are frequently ambivalent: while formally rejecting claims to traditional authoritarianism, many clergy maintain it latently in their self-image, and experience role conflict with their parishioners as a result, as Michael Daniel has pointed out.[26] This gives them an ongoing tension with laity not experienced to the same degree by clergy of other brands of churchmanship, leading to feelings of irritation and frustration at 'sheep who will not be led'.[27] Such ideological factors exacerbate the loneliness experienced by many clergy.[28]

Further, again following Daniel, recently ordained Catholic clergy appear to be peculiarly vulnerable to the ideas of current liberal theology. In addition, the Parish Communion movement has assisted a process of ideological dilution through which moderate ritual of a Catholic type has come to be associated with a variety of theological orientations. Hence Catholic externals are no longer a guarantee of any brand of Catholic orthodoxy, and are frequently unaccompanied by attempts to promulgate norms of doctrine or discipline. This is further influenced by an increasing reluctance among clergy to visit parishioners in their homes, thus diminishing the possibility of influence through personal interaction.

Thus, though virtually all the innovations for which earlier generations of Anglo-Catholics fought are now generally possible, in practice they are desired less and less by younger clergy. A simpler liturgy, the dismantling of shrines and side altars, the decline of services such as Benediction, for which a major battle was fought less than 40 years ago, less emphasis on confession and the keeping of a rule of life, are now central features of a Catholic group which sees the eucharist increasingly as a fellowship meal rather than a sacred mystery, and which accepts the Series Two Communion rite as preferable to the controversial and illegal English Missal.

Changes of this kind facilitate ecumenism (together with the increasing ritualism in nonconformity noted by Bryan Wilson and Eric Carlton),[29] but they provide fewer structural and ideological supports for the priest's role as a distinctive calling. Hence there is a decline in vocations to the priesthood; Catholic colleges experience a disproportionate drop in numbers of ordinands in the context of a general decline in clerical recruitment, and have a high drop-out rate. Some younger clergy devote much of their time to community welfare work and involvement in movements like Oxfam and Shelter, which take the place in parish life of traditional devotional societies such as the Confraternity of the Blessed Sacrament; to this extent the clergy's pastoral role is secularized. Such social involvement is, of course, part of the Catholic tradition, but whereas historically this was directly related to, and sprang from, a strong Catholic spirituality, for many of the present generation such an order of priorities is reversed or exists to a decreasing extent. In addition, full time social work, and even sociology itself, can provide something approaching a functional alternative to the priesthood for young men with social commitment who are critical of church structures and tradition.

The priest's role is thus now highly insecure. In a sense it has always been so: in the heyday of Anglo-Catholicism this insecurity derived from membership of a deviant group, in structural opposition to the established order, with a fragmented ideology and limited structural cohesion and integration, both of which made for limited role consensus and hence created deep strains and tensions. Though the Catholic party is now firmly attached to the Anglican establishment, and meets little opposition, the former weaknesses have been added to by further ideological and structural changes, both inside and outside the church, so that paradoxically, at a time when all the major battles of Anglo-Catholicism have been fought and won, the role of its priestly leadership is more unstable than ever before.

## NOTES

1. Accounts of the development of the movement may be found in Owen Chadwick, *The Victorian Church*, Part I 1966, Part II 1970, A. & C. Black; W. L. Knox, *The Catholic Movement in the Church of England*, 1923; S. L. Ollard, *Short History of the Oxford Movement*, Mowbrays 1915, and *The Anglo-Catholic Revival*, Mowbrays 1925; C. P. S. Clarke, *The Oxford Movement and After*, 1937; W. J. Sparrow-Simpson: *The History of the Catholic Revival from 1845*, Allen & Unwin 1932; D. Morse-Boycott, *The Secret Story of the Oxford Movement*, Skeffington 1933. For accounts of the more recent period see Dom Anselm Hughes, *The Rivers of the Flood*, Faith Press 1961; and John Gunstone, 'Catholics in the Church of England' in John Wilkinson (ed.), *Catholic Anglicans Today*, Darton, Longman & Todd 1968, pp. 183–203.

2. David Martin, *A Sociology of English Religion*, SCM Press and Heinemann 1967, p. 72.

3. J. Embry, *The Catholic Movement and the SSC*, Faith Press 1931, pp. 269–70.

4. J. Embry, op. cit., pp. 33–4.

5. See *inter alia* J. G. Lockhart, *Viscount Halifax, 1885–1934*, Part II, Bles 1936, p. 146, and Halifax's preface to Clifton Kelway, *The Story of the Catholic Revival*, Cope & Fenwick 1915, p.x. A similar view is trenchantly stated in the comments of one of the priests imprisoned for ritualism, S. F. Green, quoted in S. Baring-Gould, *The Church Revival*, Methuen, 2nd ed. 1914, p. 248.

6. George Orwell, 'Inside the Whale' in *Selected Essays*, Penguin 1957, p. 35.

7. My colleague Mr J. C. Newton has pointed out to me the significance of the anti-Catholic mobs of this period as evidence of a loosely constituted body of labour which could be mobilized for payment to serve the ends of interests whose goals they did not share, and their possible connection with blackleg labour used for anti-union purposes in the same period. Similarly, one of my students, Mr L. Marlow, has drawn my attention to interesting similarities with the 'Church-and-King' mobs of an earlier period.

8. On this see Chadwick, op. cit., Part II, pp. 337–8.

9. The effect of high office on clergy is discussed generally by Paul Ferris in *The Church of England*, Penguin 1964, p. 83f., and with reference to the Catholic movement by Hughes, op. cit., pp. 72–3.

10. On Temple see various comments in the *Report of the Royal Commission on Ecclesiastical Discipline*, HMSO 1906, and in the evidence on the historical development of the movement by Archbishop Randall Davidson. On Winnington-Ingram see S. C. Carpenter, *Winnington-Ingram*, Hodder 1949, who also supports the judgment on Temple's episcopate. On Mandell Creighton see W. G. Fallows, *Mandell Creighton and the English Church*, OUP 1964, especially ch. 7, 'The Ritual Cloud'.

11. Fallows, op. cit., p. 86.

12. Discussed by Carpenter, op. cit., pp. 170–5.

13. On this see Hugh Ross Williamson, *The Walled Garden*, 1956, and William Purcell, *Fisher of Lambeth*, Hodder 1969, pp. 94–5.

14. Ronald C. D. Jasper, *George Bell, Bishop of Chichester*, OUP 1967, ch. 9.

15. Morse-Boycott, op. cit., pp. 271–3.

16. Relatively recent cases such as those of Carshalton (on this see issues of the *Church Times*, July–Dec. 1959) and Castletown (items in *Church Times* 24 April and 18 May 1959 and 14 April 1960) would not seem to disprove my general point.

17. Horace Keast, 'A Catholic Notebook – VII' in *Fiery Cross*, July 1943.

18. See comments by Morse-Boycott, op. cit., p. 192; Gunstone, loc. cit., pp. 191–2; also Hughes' discussions of extremists and moderates, especially ch. 4, 'Putting on the brake'.

19. See figures quoted in the evidence of various witnesses to the 1904 Royal Commission and in R. Mudie-Smith (ed.), *The Religious Life of London*, Hodder 1904.

20. The close character of the movement is described by Gunstone, loc. cit., pp. 189–91. My comments here are intended to apply particularly to the newer Catholic parishes and those being Catholicized for the first time.

21. The Roman position on this question was definitively stated in the Papal Bull, *Apostolicae Curae*, 1896, and debate on the issue since has been voluminous. For summaries see *Infallible Fallacies: An Anglican reply to Roman Catholic Arguments* by some Priests of the Anglican Communion, 2nd ed. SPCK 1958; Francis Clark SJ, *The Catholic Church and Anglican Orders*, Catholic Truth Society 1962. A massive study has recently been published by a Roman priest who himself is a convert from Anglicanism: John Jay Hughes, *Stewards of the Lord: a reappraisal of Anglican orders*, Sheed & Ward 1970.

22. Owen Francis Dudley, 'What I Found' in John A. O'Brien (ed.), *The Road to Damascus*, Image Books 1955, p. 125. See the four volumes of this series, published in this country by W. H. Allen, for further accounts of the conversion of Anglican priests and laity; also Vernon Johnson, *One Lord, One Faith*, Sheed & Ward 1963 (first published 1929); Ronald Knox, *A Spiritual Aeneid*, Burns & Oates 1958 (first published 1918); Hugh Ross Williamson, op. cit.; Bruno Scott James, *Asking for Trouble*, Darton, Longman & Todd 1962. For an example of a conversion *away from* Catholicism, see W. Rowland Jones, *Diary of a Misfit Priest*, Allen & Unwin 1960.

23. Sandys Wason's biretta was referred to by one irreverent person as 'a tea-cosy' – Bernard Walke: *Twenty Years at St Hilary*, Methuen, 3rd ed. 1937, p. 19.

24. Walke, op. cit., p. 153.

25. See eg letter in *The Catholic Standard for Anglicans*, 3(1), January 1967, p. 5.

26. Michael Daniel: (a) 'Catholic, Evangelical and Liberal in the Anglican Priesthood', *Sociological Yearbook of Religion in Britain 1*, SCM Press 1968; (b)

'The association between churchmanship and the Anglican clergyman's self-image', *International Conference of Religious Sociology*, 1967.

27. Daniel, (a) p. 121.

28. On the loneliness of the clergy see Leslie Paul, *The Deployment and Payment of the Clergy*, Church Information Office 1964, Ch. 5.

29. Bryan Wilson, *Religion in Secular Society*, Watts & Co. 1966, pp. 136–8; Eric Carlton, 'The Predicament of the Baptist Minister', *New Society*, 7 January 1965, p. 11.

I have tried to keep citations to a minimum; the analysis in this paper is based on material from my thesis *Anglo-Catholicism: Ideology and Influence* (Ph.D. London – in progress), where far more extensive references are given. In preparing this I have drawn not only on published material, but also on a large number of interviews and discussions with Anglo-Catholic clergy and laity; in particular I would like to acknowledge the help given me by Canon Colin Stephenson, Father John Gaskell, Father John Vaughan-Jones, Father Kenneth Leech and Father Philip Gray. Needless to say, none of these should be held responsible for the opinions expressed above.

# 5 Concepts of Church Membership

*Peter L. Sissons*

## Introduction

THIS article arises out of a broadly based investigation of the significance of church membership in the culture of a Scottish industrial town. The object of the research is to investigate the socio-religious meanings of church membership within the context of criticisms which have been made of church membership as an index of religiosity, and within the context of those investigations which describe and analyse the peripheral social location of church-centred religion.

The growth of parish studies and the developing sociological interest within the institutional church, along with the emergence of the church as a potential client of the sociologist, have combined to obscure the fact that the place of the church within the sociology of religion is open to debate. Latterly the problem of the church has begun to reassert itself, and a clue to the nature of the problem may be found in the study of church membership. The meaningfulness of church membership has been raised on two broad planes. Firstly, the question has been raised in the context of the apparent rejection of institutional Christianity as the dominant religious mode in western society. On this plane it is argued that in a predominantly secular and pluralist society church membership is not and cannot be a viable index of religiosity. On the second plane the question arises differently, emerging as it does from empirical studies of the churches. In brief, the argument is that church membership alone is not a sufficient index of religiosity. In order to understand the structure and functions of religion in society it is necessary to establish categories or typologies which combine church membership with attendance regularity, subscription to religious beliefs and the various criteria of religiosity. Within such models of religiosity denominational differentials, particularly differentials within Protestantism, may become blurred and church membership may become just one, and not necessarily the essential, criterion of religiosity.

The first plane is associated with those who adopt a theoretical schema within which religion is accorded an inclusive definition[1] and with those who understand religion in functional terms and for whom the religion of the churches is not functional.[2] On this plane far-reaching questions are raised for the sociology of religion. There is a demand for the reappraisal of the subject matter of the discipline and a consideration of the problems of conceptualizing religion in their normative and methodological dimensions. The second plane is in some respects related to the first, but it rises primarily from the contingencies of research which demand that more or less arbitrary decisions concerning the nature and location of religion must be made. These decisions arise in part from frustration with the difficulties of establishing a consensus of the criteria of religious belonging adopted by the various religious institutions, and lead to the problems of framing categories of religiosity which permit an examination of religion in ways which transcend the differing ecclesiastical criteria of belonging to the church. The latter problem is sometimes manifested through the attempt to obtain a statistical measure of church membership which would be meaningful in relation to the different theological traditions, whilst at the same time being a realistic measure in terms of the official and unofficial criteria adopted by the different churches in maintaining their membership records.[3] This may lead to the minutiae of institutional belonging being discarded or ignored in favour of a multi-dimensional approach to religiosity which minimizes the importance of the different interpretations of belonging to the church[4] or discusses such belonging in terms of institutional distance correlated with degrees of subscription to the ideals of the institution.[5] In order to illuminate these latter problems it was decided to devote time to a preliminary exploration of the ways in which the members of institutions associated with several ecclesiastical traditions conceptualized church membership, both in terms of the qualities necessary for church membership and in terms of the expected differences between those who are members of a church and those who are not. This article is a description of the results of that preliminary exploration.

## The background and scope of the research

There is prevalent amongst sociologists a belief that certain broad assumptions about religion hold true for the whole of Western European society. Regardless of the individual sociologist's stance on theories of secularization there is a general acceptance of the decline of institutional religion in Western Europe, evidenced by decreasing church attendances and the reduced impact of traditional religious values upon the values and behaviour of the individual and the society. There are grounds for suggesting that Scotland, superficially at least, may be atypical. In this case the town selected for investigation, an established industrial centre with a population of rather more than 38,000, sustains 37 religious institutions. Amongst these the Church of Scotland is dominant with eleven parish churches, followed by the Roman Catholic Church which has two major church buildings along with a small hall used as a church by the town's Polish Catholic community and a Carmelite convent where a number of the Catholic population regularly attend mass. In addition to the Church of Scotland there are six other churches rooted in orthodox Protestantism along with open and closed assemblies of the Christian Brethren, various evangelical missions and Pentecostalist groups, and four Christian deviationist bodies.

At a conservative estimate, based on figures collected from the institutions and from interviews conducted with a random sample of the population, 50% of the people in the town are nominally associated with one or another of religious institutions, whilst an additional unknown percentage is associated with churches outside its boundaries. From this variety it will be seen that the town has a very representative pattern of institutional religion within the context of which a wide range of types of religiosity might be expected to develop. In view of the sampling difficulties created by the various definitions of church membership it was decided that the preliminary investigation would be confined to the elected lay leaders in those churches which were providing the focus for the major part of the research, and those were selected who had reached the highest level of responsibility in their own tradition.

The eleven churches from which the sample of lay leaders was taken were initially selected on the basis of their denominational spread; in the case of the Church of Scotland congregations, five of which were included in the sampling, the selection was on the basis of social and theological type. In addition to the Church of Scotland congregations a Roman Catholic church, the Congregational church, the Scottish Episcopal church, two open assemblies of the Christian Brethren and a non-denominational evangelistic mission were included in the investigation. Questionnaires were administered to the

Elders of the Church of Scotland congregations and to the nearest equivalent in the other churches, that is to say, to the members of the Roman Catholic Parish Council, the Episcopal Vestry members, and to the Elders of the Congregational church,[6] the two assemblies and the mission. The functions of these lay leaders, their status, the rules which controlled their election and determined the length of their tenure of office varied from church to church, as did the theological implications of their offices, but in so far as any laymen in these churches might be expected to be articulate about membership of the institution these were the ones who should be the most articulate.

A total of 256 lay leaders was approached of whom 169 finally completed the questionnaire, a response rate of 66 %. The responses from individual churches varied, and no denomination revealed a consistently high or low response. The lowest of all was from a Church of Scotland congregation and the highest was from the non-denominational mission, but there were high responses from Church of Scotland congregations and low responses from non-Church of Scotland congregations. There was no correlation between the rate of response and denomination, or rate of response and socio-economic class.

The responses were divided into three groups, the Church of Scotland, the Roman Catholic and the non-Church of Scotland Protestant. It was not intended that these should be regarded as being socio-religious groups in Lenski's sense;[7] they are convenience groupings which in the case of the first two are quite unambiguous. The third is a grouping of Congregational, Episcopalian, Evangelical and Brethren, all of which are minority bodies within the religious life of the town and which, when aggregated, remain very much a minority. The non-Church of Scotland Protestant churches, although they are many in number and varied in doctrine, nonetheless account for only about 2,000 of the population. It is proposed therefore to categorize them in one group throughout the research whilst being careful to observe and record any significant differences which may occur within that group. A problem with the analysis of data obtained from these Protestant minorities and from the Roman Catholics was the small number of responses classified in these groups. This is a problem which does not arise in the major research where a larger, more carefully controlled sample has been employed.

*Demographic and socio-economic data*

The Church of Scotland Elders constituted 76·9% of the informants; 6·5% were Roman Catholics and 16·6% were leaders in the Protestant minorities.[8] The distribution of socio-economic class in each of the three groups differed significantly. The town is characterized by a low percentage of the population in the professional and intermediate classifications used by the Registrar General and more than 50% of employed men are engaged in the skilled occupations. Only the lay leaders in the non-Church of Scotland Protestant churches approximated to this distribution. The leadership in the Church of Scotland congregations is in the hands of middle-class men. Less than 1% of the Elders in the five Church of Scotland congregations were partly-skilled or unskilled men.

Who were the leaders? Three of the Church of Scotland informants were bank managers, several were directors of large companies, whilst industrial and works chemists reflect the local industrial interests. Twelve of the Church of Scotland Elders were in the teaching profession, three of them being headmasters. Other Elders included a retired prison governor, several solicitors, accountants, architects and local government officials. Amongst the non-Church of Scotland Protestant churches only the Episcopal church had a professional informant, whilst only the non-denominational mission had an informant classified as an unskilled worker. None of the Catholics was in the Registrar General's professional classification, although 46% of the Catholic informants were engaged in the intermediate occupations as teachers, insurance agents and sales representatives. All the Church of Scotland Elders were men, compared with 96% of the non-Church of Scotland Protestant leaders and 64% of the Catholics.[9] The Catholics were the youngest of the lay leaders: all of them were under 56 years of age, compared with 57% of the non-Church of Scotland Protestants and 49% of the Church of Scotland Elders.

*Qualities essential to church membership*

The lay leaders were asked two questions relevant to their understanding of church membership. It was not expected that the responses to these questions would provide mutually exclusive categories of religious belonging, ready-made for the use of the sociologist. It was the intention to try to derive from the responses strands of meaning and insights which could be examined in relation to the three groups and which would provide guide-lines for the construction of an interview schedule to be used for the intensive interviewing of a sample of church members and a control group of non-church members. As the composition of the three religious groups differed in statistically significant ways it was also decided to explore the association between understandings of church membership and socio-economic class. The two questions which were put to the informants were:

(*a*) Give in order of importance no more than five of the qualities which you consider to be most desirable in a member of the Christian Church.

(*b*) Give in order of importance no more than five ways in which you think that church members should differ from non-church members.

The responses to the two questions will first of all be examined separately.

The responses made by the Church of Scotland Elders and the members of the Roman Catholic Parish Council were focused for the most part upon broad moral qualities. Sincerity, decency, loyalty, modesty, integrity, were amongst the one word responses used to describe the necessary qualities of church membership, whilst other responses elaborated upon these. Those who specifically referred to distinctively 'religious' qualities were in a minority. A bank manager who was a member of an upper-middle-class parish church was fairly exceptional amongst the Church of Scotland informants in that amongst the qualities of church membership he included 'belief in God' and 'faith'. One of the more unusual Roman Catholic responses was that of a machinist in a clothing factory who cited 'a willingness to work for Christ' as one of the qualities of church membership. More often the qualities detailed were moral abstractions with a universal application indicative of a rather austere virtuousness. Religious and theological distinctions did not occur in these responses, which for the most part were little different from the conventional ethical values which underlie most of Western society. This compares with the results obtained by Donald Robertson when he asked a sample of men in a district of Edinburgh to say 'What a Christian is'.[10] Those specifically religious values which occurred in the responses were broadly based and might be summed up in the response of a retired insurance salesman, a Church of Scotland Elder, who described as a major quality of the church member 'one's complete faith in one's own religious beliefs, whatever they may be'. By contrast the responses from the leaders in the Protestant minorities were characterized by their direct references to Christian criteria of religious identity, particularly those criteria associated with pietism. A church member must be 'born again'; he must be 'converted to Christ'; he must have 'personally accepted Christ as his saviour'; and in this state of redemption he must be 'Christlike in all his actions', 'obedient to God's revealed truths' and 'committed to the furtherance of the gospel'. These qualities were often qualified by others which were more practical and specific. A middle-aged iron moulder, an Elder in the non-denominational mission, expanded his emphasis upon biblical belief with the further essential quality that church members should be 'pleasant in their approach to others', whilst a Brethren businessman included 'straightforward dealings' and 'moral living and talking' after 'conversion' and 'real conviction of belief'. These responses were more characteristic of the sectarian informants included in this group, but they were not exclusive to the Brethren and the evangelicals, and occasionally the sect leaders focused upon moral behaviour and general virtues. Religious responses were, however, in the majority, and they were pietistic and exclusive in character, emphasizing a qualifying experience such as conversion, rebirth or believers' baptism.

The content of the responses was separated into eight broad categories for analysis.

1. *Attitudes towards others* Attitudes towards other people had a high place in the responses of all three groups but they were particularly emphasized by the Church of Scotland and Roman Catholic informants. For the most part these attitudes were characterized by liberal, universalistic qualities; friendliness, tolerance and brotherly love, and they are best summed up in a sentence written by one of the Church of Scotland Elders: 'The church member will have a generally good attitude towards his fellow men.'

2. *Moral characteristics* The moral characteristics ascribed to the church member were generally of two kinds: those which named a single abstract moral virtue, 'honesty' or 'humility' for example, and those which were cast in a behavioural context and which were occasionally phrased negatively, 'the church member will avoid all gambling', and 'the church member will not engage in permissiveness'. 31·5% of all the Church of Scotland responses and 41% of all the Roman Catholic responses were in this general category.

3. *Specifically religious characteristics* These responses were those which drew upon specifically religious sentiments, or used language which was unambiguously 'religious' in character. The responses of the informants from the sects described above were coded in this category, as was the response of a Church of Scotland Elder who wrote: 'The church member will live under and with God's good grace.' An examination of these responses revealed no significant doctrinal differences; for the most part they tended to emphasize belief, belief in Jesus Christ, acceptance of God's Word, and transforming effects of faith upon the personality.

4. *Devotional and evangelical activities* One group of responses stood out as referring to specific and pietistic interpretations of religious behaviour. Qualities of the church member included 'regular prayer', 'daily use of the bible in the home', coupled with quite specific evangelical responsibilities, 'winning others for Christ' and 'proclaiming the gospel'. These responses were mainly characteristic of the Brethren.

5. *Financial giving* The giving of money, the raising of money and the administration, decision making and planning associated with income and expenditure inevitably play a large part in the life of all the churches and particularly in the life of the lay leaders. Surprisingly, finance figured very little in the responses made by the informants. None of the Catholics mentioned the giving of money, but a number of the Protestants referred to 'Christian liberality', and it was decided to place this small number of responses in a separate category, partly because the emphasis upon money is quite often used as a source of criticism of the churches, and partly because the giving of money to the institution may be cited as a measure of the individual's commitment to its goals and values.

6. *Attitudes towards the church* In addition to the giving of money other positive attitudes towards the church were mentioned as being qualities desirable in a church member. Some of these responses referred to participation in church activities other than worship but for the most part the focus was upon regularity of attendance at worship and more emphasis was given to this by the Protestants than by the Catholics.

7. *Cognitive attitudes* A number of lay leaders made their responses in relatively sophisticated language in which they suggested that a fairly high level of intellectual comprehension should be required of the church member. The actual content of these responses

varied. Some were concerned with a universal or cosmological dimension whilst others made intellectual statements about Christ and about belief. The Catholic manager of a multiple store wrote, 'the member of the church should possess a realistic appreciation of the church's role as an integral part of society in the modern world'.

8. *Tolerance*   Tolerance of other churches and denominations was included amongst the responses of a small number of informants. There were relatively few of these but as they may reflect the extent of the influence of an ecumenical mood within the churches they were separated into a category.

Each of these categories transcended the boundaries which divided the three sub-samples. There was no characteristically Catholic or characteristically Calvinist distinction between the Catholic and Church of Scotland informants, and with the exception of the Brethren the data did not cluster in any obvious way about institutional variables.

The ordering of the responses in the five positions of importance proved to have little statistical significance when considered in relation to membership of the three groups and to socio-economic class, although associations were found between the importance ascribed to specifically religious characteristics and denominational affiliation; and between the importance ascribed to participation in devotional and evangelical activities and those lay leaders of all three groups who had been classified in the non-manual category of the Registrar General's classification of skilled occupations.

The order of importance was provisionally discarded as a factor in the analysis and attention was focused upon the number of times the qualities in each category were mentioned in the responses. As a result a rather clearer picture began to emerge. The Roman Catholic Parish Council and the Church of Scotland Elders appeared to be closely aligned in their responses, whilst the non-Church of Scotland Protestant leaders were set apart by their choices. The Church of Scotland Elders and the Catholic leaders mentioned moral characteristics of church membership most frequently, followed closely by responses indicative of attitudes towards others. By contrast the non-Church of Scotland Protestants emphasized those qualities broadly categorized as religious. The two Protestant groups were nearest to each other when they cited attitudes towards the church and financial giving as qualities of church membership. The differences between the three groups were significant at the 0·01 level.

In order to summarize the similarities and differences which were statistically significant an index of dissimilarity was used, of the type found in the paper by Leonard Broom and Norval D. Glenn.[11] The simple nature and function of this is perhaps best described in their words; '. . . an index of dissimilarity (ID) is used as a summary measure of the differences between each pair of compared religious categories . . . The value of the index is simply the percentage of respondents of either religion who would have to change their responses in order for the response distributions to be identical.' When this simple measure was applied to the total distribution of qualities of church membership through the three groups the following range of dissimilarity was found.

Church of Scotland/Roman Catholic ID     =    3·73
Church of Scotland/Protestant Minorities ID =    5·15
Roman Catholic/Protestant Minorities ID     =    7·85

Whilst this is a rough measure it nonetheless illustrates how the Church of Scotland and Roman Catholic groups are more in alignment than any of the other possible pairings of sub-samples.

The major differences between the socio-economic classes occurred with regard to belief and other religious qualities; participation in devotional and evangelical activities; financial giving; cognitive statements; and tolerance of other denominations and churches. The responses made by those in the first three of the Registrar General's classifications were concerned primarily with moral characteristics and attitudes towards other people, whilst the emphasis of the responses made by those in Classes IV and V was upon religious qualities, devotionalism and evangelism. Financial giving and cognitive statements were accorded little importance, but in as much as they were given importance it was ascribed to them by informants belonging to the professional classification.

The above analysis is based on data which were originally ordered in a complicated manner in terms of their identification with a particular category of qualities and a particular order of priorities. They were simplified numerically by eliminating the order of priorities as a factor in the analysis with the result that the differences and similarities became clearer. In order to illustrate the apparent alignment between the Church of Scotland and Roman Catholic informants even more clearly the process of simplification was taken a stage further. The data were polarized, divided into those data indicative of specifically religious qualities, those in which Christianity, its teachings, the church, belief, devotional activity, evangelism, prayer and faith were made explicit, and into those data in which the religious content was implicit, those responses which did not specifically refer to religious forms, but which focused upon abstractions, dictates of behaviour or attitude. The data ordered in these broad categories were then examined against the denominational affiliation and socioeconomic class of the informants. The resulting alignment of religion and class can be seen in the table below. It should be underscored that the number of responses in Classes IV and V are small, and that in Class V they are too small to be accorded statistical significance.

## TABLE ONE

'Non-religious' qualities cited more often than 'religious'

| Church of Scotland | 66·29% | Class | I | Professional | 80·09% |
|---|---|---|---|---|---|
| Roman Catholic | 76·56% | | II | Intermediate | 73·20% |
| | | | III | Skilled Non-Manual | 51·70% |
| | | | III | Skilled Manual | 62·43% |

'Religious' qualities cited more often than 'non-religious'

| Brethren, Congrega- | | Class | IV | Partly Skilled | 60% |
|---|---|---|---|---|---|
| tional, Episcopal and | | | V | Unskilled | 80% |
| Non-denominational | 51·9% | | | | |

The relationship between the three religious groups when the distribution of qualities is polarized can again be measured in terms of the index of dissimilarity.

Church of Scotland/Roman Catholic ID $=$ 10·17
Church of Scotland/Protestant Minorities ID $=$ 18·26
Roman Catholic/Protestant Minorities ID $=$ 28·43

The significance of the alignment between the Church of Scotland and Roman Catholic informants will be returned to as the differences postulated between church members and non-church members are considered.

*Qualitative differences between church members and*
*non-church members*

The second question asked of the informants was: 'Give in order of importance no more than five ways in which you think that church members should differ from non-church members.'

This question caused considerable unease amongst the Church of Scotland informants. This unease may have been the result of the phrasing of the question. A number of the Church of Scotland Elders were troubled by the words 'should differ'. The unease experienced over the phrasing is itself indicative of a tension which some of the Elders articulated in their responses to the question, a tension arising out of their uncertainty about the relationship between church and society. A 33-year-old quantity surveyor said: 'Personally I do not think church members and non-church members do differ in as many as five ways. There are probably people who do not attend church who are better Christians than I am. If a man does his duty to his family and to his employer he is acting as a Christian, and therefore I don't think we can say he is any different from someone who may be a church member but a layabout – except that he is a better man.' The general manager of a large trade federation wrote tersely against the question; 'Can *you* describe a non-church member?', whilst a retired hairdresser commented quite simply: 'Should there be a difference? We are all God's children.' Implicit within these responses is the universalism which led to the citing of broad moral characteristics as qualities of church membership. On the one hand this universalism is expressed ethically. Ethical values are superior to religious belonging and are more important in the evaluation of another human being, consequently criteria of church membership take second place to these universal qualities. 'I know many non-church members who are *better* than church members'; 'This question smacks of holier than thou'; 'You are suggesting in this question that church members are superior to non-church members', were typical of some of the responses provoked by this question. On the other hand this universalism is expressed in the feeling that there are no significant qualitative differences between church members and non-church members, as expressed in the phrase: 'We are all God's children.'

The remaining responses to this question fell into six categories comparable with the eight categories suggested by the responses to the first question. These were divided as follows:

1. *Moral differences* These were differences of broad moral values directly comparable with the moral qualities cited in response to the first question. The Roman Catholics particularly cited moral differences between church members and non-church members and they frequently did so by referring to their selection of qualities of church membership with the comment: 'The church member will show the above more clearly than the non-church member.'

2. *Behavioural differences with no specific religious content* The church member will behave differently in society from the non-church member, usually as the upholder of conventional morality. A 64-year-old Church of Scotland draughtsman wrote: 'The church member will not be given to boasting or swearing or evil speaking ... he will take no part in gambling, coupons, premium bonds etc.' 'In his life he will express responsibility for others', wrote a Roman Catholic local government officer. The values implicit within the behaviour may be the same as those of the non-church member, but the church member will pursue them with greater rigour, he will express more emphatically in his behaviour the *mores* to which the whole society subscribes. Consequently there is considerable emphasis by Roman Catholic and Church of Scotland informants upon behavioural example. In his daily life the church member will express more clearly than the non-church member the abstract qualities of honesty, charity, integrity. 'Greater than . . .', 'better than . . .', 'more than . . .', were regular prefaces to the responses coded in this category. A senior member of the Episcopal Vestry said that the church member would have 'a greater sense of responsibility', 'better ability to help others', and that he would be 'better informed about his civic duties'; whilst a Congregational layman said that the church member would differ from the non-church member 'by deed and action'. These differences, in which no specific religious content is identified, are not so much qualitative differences as reflections of higher degrees of commitment to or involvement in the behavioural expression of universal values.

3. *Behavioural differences with a specific religious content* These differences include devotional practice, evangelism and also those activities indicative of a specifically Christian world view. A Church of Scotland headmaster wrote: 'The church member will differ from the non-church member in the daily practice of a Christian believer', whilst a bank manager wrote that 'The church member will live in accordance with Christ's teaching.' The responses in these categories

were made for the most part by the Protestants in both groups, and were the only responses in which the traditional Protestant ethic was really made explicit.

4. *Attitudinal differences with no religious content* These responses ostensibly claimed that the church member would be in possession of values which differ from the values of the non-church member. In fact these attitudes were really more intense versions of secular attitudes, accompanied once again by the prefaces 'greater than . . .', 'more than . . .', and 'better than . . .'.

5. *Attitudinal differences with a religious content* In this category the differences between church members and non-church members are unambiguous in that the attitude of the church member by virtue of belief or faith may be the antithesis of the attitude of the non-church member. Such attitudes would be characterized by 'love for God's Word and God's house', 'the recognition of Jesus as Saviour and Lord'. The largest percentage of responses in this category is taken up by the non-Church of Scotland Protestants, although Roman Catholic and Church of Scotland informants have a relatively high rate of response within this category.

6. *Religious differences of a cognitive nature* These differences are similar to the cognitive attitudes categorized as qualities of church membership. The highest percentage coded in this category belonged to the non-Church of Scotland Protestant group. Typical of these was the response of an Episcopalian, a retired mechanical engineer, who wrote that the church member would differ from the non-church member in that he would have 'an understanding of the spiritual reality underlying the affairs of the world'.

The importance ascribed to these categories differed significantly when it was examined in association with religious group and socio-economic class. The Roman Catholics accorded most importance to moral differences and behavioural differences without a specific religious content. The non-Church of Scotland Protestant informants accorded highest importance to the behavioural differences with a specific religious content, the attitudinal differences with a specific religious content and the religious differences of a cognitive type. In most instances the percentage differences were quite striking, and the differences in each of these categories were significant at the 0·001 level.

The data illustrate that not only do the non-Church of Scotland Protestant informants ascribe the greatest priority to those responses with a religious content, by giving them first and second orders of importance, but that also they mention such differences more often. The Church of Scotland or Catholic informants might place one or another of the religious differences in first or second position, but they will then go on to make responses of a moral or behavioural kind, whereas the non-Church of Scotland Protestants would go on to place religious differences in third, fourth and fifth positions of importance. This is consistent with the response to the ordering of religious qualities of church membership.

There were no statistically significant differences between the five socio-economic classes in the way they ordered their responses to this question. Membership of a religious group was emphatically more significant than class in the priority given to the differences postulated between church members and non-church members.

The differences were then correlated with the religious groups on the basis of the number of responses within each category, regardless of priority and regardless of the number of informants. As with the previous questions this served to clarify the nature of the differences between the three religious groups, and once again the overall alignment was between the Church of Scotland and Roman Catholic informants who stood over against the non-Church of Scotland Protestants. The only category in which there was a clear degree of similarity between the Protestant groups was that on behavioural differences with a religious content, 23·6% and 26·1% respectively. As a summary the index of dissimilarity was used.

Church of Scotland/Roman Catholic ID = 4·5
Church of Scotland/Protestant Minorities ID = 5·4
Roman Catholic/Protestant Minorities ID = 9·5

The first factor to emerge is the clear evidence that the non-Church of Scotland lay leaders, usually but not exclusively the sectarians, consistently offered a self-consciously religious response. In this they were different from both the Church of Scotland and the Roman Catholic informants. The Church of Scotland informants were consistently aligned with the Roman Catholics but many Church of Scotland responses were clearly similar to those of the evangelicals amongst the other Protestants. A 53-year-old Coal Board engineer, an Elder in the most intellectual of the five Church of Scotland congregations, described the differences between church members and non-church members as being the church members' 'inward happiness that they have found Christ, and their humbleness in their inability to 'sell' him to others'; and a 35-year-old probation officer wrote 'the church member will have a personal commitment to Jesus Christ'. The largest number of responses from the Church of Scotland and Catholic leaders was coded in the category of behavioural differences with no specific religious content, after which the two groups deviated, the Church of Scotland informants joining with their Protestant colleagues in their emphasis upon behavioural differences with a religious content, whilst the Roman Catholics emphasized moral differences. The differences between the Church of Scotland Elders and the Catholic Parish Council members seem to be that whilst the former regard the major differences as being behavioural, the latter regard them as being moral and behavioural without religious content. The high level of similarity between these two groups in other categories minimizes the differences between them. The differences between church members and non-church members cited by the Church of Scotland informants and the Roman Catholics are differences of intensity rather than differences which reflect antithetical cultures. When differences are placed in the moral or non-religious behavioural categories it is not that the church member necessarily subscribes to a different moral code or behaves in a different manner; it is that the church member is expected to be exemplary in his acceptance of a moral code which is regarded as being universal within the culture, whilst his behaviour is the successful pursuit of behavioural standards culturally accepted and subscribed to by the whole community. The behavioural differences with a religious content favoured by Church of Scotland informants also tend to be differences of achievement rather than differences of values. The significance of religious motivation is that it enables the church member to achieve that which is culturally desirable for all. It is this feeling which probably caused so much embarrassment amongst the Church of Scotland informants as they contemplated this question. They did not want to say that church members were better than, more exemplary than, superior to, and yet this seemed to be the only possible range of differences which could exist between church members and non-church members. The non-Church of Scotland Protestants, particularly the sectarians, were more inclined to see a cultural difference between the church member and the non-church member. The differences they cited were indicative of a difference between those who belonged to a religious culture and those who did not.

When the total number of responses was correlated with socio-economic class, disregarding the order of importance, the most distinctive and statistically significant feature was the way in which skilled non-manual workers emphasized differences with specifically religious characteristics, whether behavioural or attitudinal, compared with informants in partly-skilled occupations who emphasized attitudinal differences of a religious nature.

As with the qualities of church membership the differences between church members and non-church members were polarized, distinguishing between those responses with an explicit religious content and those in which religion was implicit. The ensuing alignment between religious groups and socio-economic class can be examined in the table below. When this table is compared with the previous one it can be seen that a higher percentage of informants expressed religious differences between church members and non-church members compared with those who emphasized religious qualities as being essential to church membership. It can also be observed that the socio-economic classes re-align themselves in their responses to the second question.

TABLE TWO

'Non-religious' differences mentioned more often than 'religious'

| Church of Scotland | 55·27% | Class I | Professional | 55·9% |
| Roman Catholic | 66·14% | II | Intermediate | 58·0% |
| | | V | Unskilled | 50·0% |

'Religious' differences mentioned more often than 'Non-religious'

| Brethren, Congrega-tional, Episcopal and Non-denominational | 67·51% | Class III | Skilled Non-Manual | 73·3% |
| | | III | Skilled Manual | 53·7% |
| | | IV | Partly Skilled | 64·0% |
| | | V | Unskilled | 50·0% |

The indices of dissimilarity compare with those relevant to the first table. Once more the similarity between the Church of Scotland and Roman Catholic informants is underlined whilst the distance between them and the non-Church of Scotland Protestants has increased.

Church of Scotland/Roman Catholic ID          =     10·87
Church of Scotland/Protestant Minorities ID  =     22·78
Roman Catholic/Protestant Minorities ID       =     32·40

## Conclusion

The investigation upon which the above description is based was a preliminary exploration of factors which might be relevant to a much larger, more comprehensive study involving an extended period of participant observation and the administration of an intensive, carefully structured interview schedule. At the outset of this paper it was stated that the purpose of the investigation was to try to uncover strands of meaning which would serve the purposes of the wider research. Accepting then that the conclusions to be drawn can be little more than hypotheses, what can be said about the understanding of church membership which emerged?

Two broad meanings of church membership are evident. In the first, membership of the church was taken to be membership of a sub-culture which was engaged in seeking to become the antithesis of a wider, national culture. Membership involves subscription to distinctive norms, the pursuit of distinctive life styles, and particularly the possession of distinctive beliefs. There is a cultural difference between the church member and the non-church member, and by implication between church and society, which is measurable in terms of religious variables. Those who ascribed this meaning to church membership were predominantly, although not exclusively, the lay leaders of the non-Church of Scotland Protestant group.

In the second meaning the church member is seen to be the member of an elitist group which embodies in exemplary form the highest ideals and values of the society. There is no cultural difference between church and society and between the church member and the non-church member. This position was adopted predominantly but not exclusively by the lay leaders of the Roman Catholic Church and the Church of Scotland.

The association between the three religious groups and the interpretations of church membership suggests that an explanation may be found through a consideration of the church/sect dichotomy and the related concepts of universalism and pietism, or inclusivism and exclusivism. Whilst the classical study by Troeltsch[12] and the early work of Niebuhr[13] may help to explain the emergence of the attitudes towards church membership which have been discussed, they are less useful for describing these attitudes. There are two reasons for this. The first is that although the two general interpretations of church membership tend to predominate in one or other of the groups in a

statistically significant manner, the interpretations nonetheless transcend the boundaries which exist between the groups. The second
reason is historical. The Church of Scotland and the Roman Catholic
Church are the two dominant religious bodies in Scotland and they
embody in Scottish society the institutionalized forms of the two
major historical alternatives which have been available to the Scottish
people, Calvinism and Catholicism. Each of these churches embodies
a rich and diverse social, religious and cultural tradition. Each, in its
own way, has succeeded in creating a unity out of diversity. The
Church of Scotland achieved its unity out of a diversity of Calvinist
bodies, many of them with firmly entrenched theological and political
opinions. This Presbyterian unity was achieved and to some extent is
maintained at the cost of constitutional and procedural tidiness. The
Roman Catholic Church in Scotland, in common with branches of
that church in many Western and non-Latin countries, embraces a
variety of sub-cultures and ethnic minorities. In Scotland, the Irish,
Italian and Polish Catholics of differing generations are variously
merged with the more or less indigenous Catholicism which originates
in the Highlands and Islands. In embracing such variety these two
major churches have established for themselves a communal form of
religious identity which is closely related to Scottish national identity.
The Catholics, it may be hypothesized, have sought acculturation
through subscription to the Calvinist norms which have prevailed in
Scottish secular institutions. The Church of Scotland, particularly in
modern times, has become in part a 'nation substitute',[14] a form of
universalism which in some senses is greater than the religious universalism implicit within its doctrine and structures. These forms of
ecclesiastical universalism clearly influence the universalism implicit
within some of the interpretations of church membership, but it is a
universalism which must be set alongside the ways in which the individual relates to the institution and the meanings which membership
of the institution may have for him. These may be related to the historical identity of the congregation or parish to which he belongs.
Expressed in the form of a simple paradigm, the church member may
place a sectarian interpretation upon his membership of a universal
institution, or an associational interpretation upon his membership
of a communal organization. Support for this is given by the sociological peculiarities of religious minorities in Scotland. The Scottish
Episcopal Church for instance, ideally a church type institution with
complementary structures, possesses many characteristics which are

typical of the sects in their associations with minorities and social deviance. Although the Episcopal Church in Scotland is traditionally a high church, liaison with the Protestant minority churches and with the Brethren is by no means uncommon. The Episcopal church included in this study has close ties with the Brethren through its organizations, and individual Episcopalians attend evening worship at a Brethren Assembly from time to time.

Denominational differentials are important for the concept of church membership, but they may be transcended by the ways in which the individual interprets his membership. On the basis of the data it is not possible to construct an exhaustive model of ideal types of church membership, but by examining the data in the light of Richard Niebuhr's analysis of the relationship between *Christ and Culture*[15] it is possible to suggest the nature of some of the components of a conceptual model of church membership which might be explored in relation to denominational differentials. Such a model would begin with two basic ideal types arising out of the two polarized alternatives in the church/society relationship. These types might be defined as the cultural and the sub-cultural, characterized by either a broad orientation to the cultural, social, ethical and economic values implicit within society or by a desire to posit a religious alternative to these values. The first type would see no essential difference between the church member and the other members of society; the major characteristics of the church member would lie in his fulfilment of the moral and conventional codes with a higher degree of application and with greater success than his non-church member counterpart. Religion would be seen in behavioural terms, in action and relationship, in which the legitimate values and aspirations of the society are upheld and pursued. The second type of church member would see the church as being primarily a community of believers for whom belief was the all important and distinctive feature of belonging to the community. Membership would be characterized by 'regeneration', 'conversion', believer's baptism, or the deliberate and self-conscious decision to join the church or to be confirmed. The church would be the major arbiter of values and norms. A third broad type would mediate between these antithetical types. The church member as transformer or conversionist, who interprets his membership of the church in terms of an intermediary role between church and society. This can be seen in the transformation of social values, ethics and beliefs or, within the cultural understanding of religion, the church member might be concerned to transform the church, either making it more cultural in its attempt to relate to society, more integrated with society, 'more relevant'; or making it more religious and less cultural, calling it back to apparently discarded biblical ideals, to greater purity in worship or church order. A similar form may be found within the narrower religious interpretation of church membership. Individual members of a Brethren Assembly, for example, may place a more cultural interpretation upon their membership and may be positing greater cultural integration, particularly in social work and in association with secular relief agencies, but also in leisure areas where they might seek to sanction attendance at concerts and the watching of television.

The major criticisms of church membership as an indicator of religiosity tend to emerge, either implicitly or explicitly, from theoretical discussions of the relationship between the religious and the secular. The sociologist's stance on the meaning of secularization will influence his interpretation of the nature and meaning of church membership. Implicit within this article is an understanding of the relationship between the religious and the secular which rejects what the writer considers to be a too facile interpretation of the churches as embodiments of middle-class values and middle-class culture. Those criticisms of the emphasis placed upon the church in the sociology of religion which arise from empirical evidence, the minority characteristics of religious populations and the non-functional nature of church-centred religion, are open to question in the town where the investigation is being conducted, and we may hypothesize that they are open to question in Scotland as a whole. It is this hypothesis that the substantive research may help to clarify.

### NOTES

1. Thomas Luckmann, *The Invisible Religion*, Macmillan, New York 1967.

2. P. H. Vrijhof, 'Methodologische Problems der Religionssoziologie', *International Yearbook for the Sociology of Religion*, Vol. II, 1967, p. 31.

3. For a full discussion of this problem and an attempted solution, see A. E. C. W. Spencer, *Notes Towards a Statistical Definition of Belonging to the Church* (a paper delivered to the International Conference on Religious Sociology, July 1962).

4. These are almost too numerous to mention, and certainly they will be well known to readers of the Yearbook. Specific reference might be made to C. Y. Glock and Rodney Stark, *Religion and Society in Tension*, Rand McNally 1965; Gerhard Lenski, *The Religious Factor*, Doubleday 1963; and to the treatment of religiosity in the Independent Television Authority's study of *Religion in Britain and Northern Ireland: A Survey of Popular Attitudes*, ITA 1970.

5. J. H. Fichter, *Social Relations in the Urban Parish*, Chicago University Press 1954.
A good example of an adaptation of Fichter's model is to be found in W. W. Schroeder and V. Obenhaus, *Religion in American Culture*, Free Press 1964.

6. Congregationalism in Scotland is structured differently from Congregationalism in England and Wales. It is complicated by the historical evolution of local congregations. The Congregational Church included in the research has its roots in the Evangelical Union tradition, and it makes a distinction between 'Elders' and 'Managers' whose functions are combined in the office of 'Deacon' in English and Welsh Congregationalism.

7. Lenski, op. cit.

8. Space prevents a discussion of the representative nature of this distribution but the discrepancy between Catholics and non-Church of Scotland Protestants is in part explained by the fact that the Catholic sub-sample is drawn from only one institution whilst the non-Church of Scotland Protestant sub-sample is drawn from five institutions.

9. Approval for the ordination of women Elders was given by the General Assembly of the Church of Scotland only one year before this investigation was conducted.

10. D. R. Robertson, 'The Relationship of Church and Class in Scotland', *A Sociological Yearbook of Religion in Britain 1*, ed. David Martin, SCM Press 1968.

11. Leonard Broom and Norval D. Glenn, 'Religious Differences in Reported Attitudes and Behaviour', *Sociological Analysis*, Vol. 27, No. 4, Winter 1966.

12. Ernst Troeltsch, *The Social Teaching of the Christian Churches*, trs. Olive Wyon, Allen & Unwin 1931.

13. H. R. Niebuhr, *The Social Sources of Denominationalism*, The Shoestring Press, New York 1929.

14. See Ian Henderson, *Scotland: Kirk and People*, Lutterworth Press 1969.

15. H. R. Niebuhr, *Christ and Culture*, Faber 1952.

I wish to acknowledge my debt to Sally Herring, who bore the main burden of processing and analysing the data described in this article.

# 6 The Bruderhof in England: a Chapter in the History of a Utopian Sect[1]

## John Whitworth

PERHAPS the most fruitful elaboration of the church-sect dichotomy established by Troeltsch has been the typology of sects developed by B. R. Wilson in two articles published in 1959 and 1963.[2] In the earlier article Wilson proposed the criterion of the sect's 'response to the world' as the basis of his taxonomy, and distinguished four types of sect; conversionist, adventist, introversionist and gnostic. In the second article Wilson extended his typology in an attempt to render it useful for the analysis of sectarian movements on the fringes of, or outside, the Christian tradition, and added three types; thaumaturgical, reformist and utopian sects.

The present article consists of an account of one stage in the development of a utopian group – the rarest and most complex of the various types of sect.

The response to the world of a utopian sect is to withdraw from the world in order that the sectarians may establish a form of society which they believe is God's blueprint for the future world order. The members of a utopian sect isolate themselves from the world in order to cultivate their spirituality and perfect their social arrangements, but they also conceive themselves to be heralds commissioned to announce the inauguration of the perfect society on earth. They try to avoid contamination by the world but, seeking to excel the world, they seek also to demonstrate their excellence, confident that all but the most corrupt of individuals will be irresistibly attracted to their society.

The belief system of a utopian sect thus sanctions a dual commitment; to isolation and to evangelization. Of these two components of the response of the sect to the world, isolation is logically prior to evangelization since it is the condition of the development of that degree of spiritual and social perfection which the sectarians believe will guarantee the spread of the divine form of society throughout the earth. In practice, however, both commitments are likely to claim the attention of the sectarians at any one period, and emphasis on one form of commitment tends to counteract the effects of prior concentration on the other.

Extreme isolation inhibits proselytization, while successful evangelization threatens the doctrinal purity and stability of the group. Consequently, the development of a utopian sect is characterized by alternate periods of emphasis on purificatory withdrawal and emphasis on evangelization. Further, failure to achieve the ultimate goal of world-transformation may at each period be explained by reference to prior over-concentration on the other form of commitment. The dual ideological emphasis is thus an inbuilt area of strategic ambiguity. The leaders of a utopian sect have a considerable degree of flexibility in their choice of policy and each choice can, at least temporarily, be legitimated in terms of the mission of the sect, and of the religious beliefs which underlie this mission.

### Development of the Bruderhof before 1935

The pacifist, communistic, communitarian sect known formally as 'The Society of Brothers' and, more colloquially, as 'the Bruderhof', today consists of three communities in the eastern United States which together have a population of about 1,000. In the half-century of its existence, the sect has at various times also established now defunct communities in Germany, Liechtenstein, England, Paraguay and Uruguay.

Any attempt to provide a full discussion of the extremely complex history, ideology and social structure of the sect would necessarily exceed present limitations of space, and would range beyond the intended scope of this Yearbook.[3] However, in order to render the following account of the Bruderhof in England intelligible, it is necessary to provide a summary discussion of the origins and early development of the sect.

The nucleus of the Bruderhof was a communitarian group which was established in 1920 at Sannerz in Hesse, Germany, by Eberhard Arnold, who remained the unchallenged leader of the sect until his death in 1935. Arnold was born in 1883 in Königsberg, East Prussia, in a Lutheran academic family. As an adolescent he was intensely religious, and at University he studied theology with a view to entering the Lutheran Church, but in 1908, after contact with radical

Baptist evangelists, Arnold concluded that those churches which con-
doned infant baptism were on a 'wrong footing', and consequently he
decided against entering the Lutheran ministry.

Arnold married in 1909, and in the years before the First World
War he lectured to a variety of inter-denominational evangelical
groups. On the outbreak of the war Arnold was called to his reserve
unit, but he received a medical discharge after short service with a
transport corps. In 1915, he accepted a post as literary director of the
German Christian Student Union, and in this capacity was responsible for the distribution of nationalistic inspirational material to
servicemen and prisoners of war. In the course of his work, Arnold
paid many visits to hospitals and to the families of servicemen, and he
became increasingly aware of the variation in the treatment received
by different ranks, and in the impact of the war on their families.[4]

Arnold's wartime experiences greatly increased his existing conviction of the corruption of the German upper classes and bourgeoisie
and, after the Armistice, his interpretation of his duty as a Christian
became more radical. In 1919, at a conference of the Christian Student Union, Arnold insisted on the 'unconditional absoluteness' of
the Sermon on the Mount, and condemned the inadequacy of denominational translations of Christian principles. Subsequently, he
asserted that all true Christians should be complete pacifists, and
should refuse to act as minions of the state in any way.

In the immediate post-war period, Arnold's dissatisfaction with
bourgeois society grew steadily deeper, but throughout 1919 he could
not decide upon a concrete alternative to middle-class life. Despite
their age, he and his wife regarded themselves as members of the Free
German Youth Movement, and they shared fully in the romantic
notions of rural life, and the nostalgia for the vanished 'folk community' which imbued the non-political youth movements of the
period.[5]

By late 1919, study of the Acts of the Apostles had convinced the
Arnolds that any truly Christian community should be based on economic communism. In the spring of the following year, at another
conference of the Christian Student Union, Arnold experienced the
Quaker form of silent meeting, a version of which still forms the
'inmost' ceremony of the Bruderhof.[6] A more concrete influence on
Arnold's conception of the new life was provided by a visit to a communistic agricultural settlement, the 'Habertshof', which had been
founded in 1919 by radical Lutherans.[7]

In the summer of 1920, a gift of 30,000 marks enabled the Arnolds and five other adults to take a ten-year lease on a house and farm at Sannerz, and to establish what they believed to be the nucleus of the coming kingdom of God on earth:

> . . . a spiritual mission of the gospel and the church of Jesus Christ, a mission station right in the middle of a Germany, a central Europe that was pagan and yet under the visitation of God.[8]

Eberhard Arnold believed himself to be commissioned by God to proclaim the continuing relevance of certain passages of scripture (especially the Sermon on the Mount), and to establish and promulgate a form of society based uncompromisingly on Christ's teachings. He did not attempt to establish a comprehensive or distinctive theology, but his somewhat vague and eclectic religious writings were deeply influenced by the 'neo-orthodox' theology which was elaborated in Germany after the First World War. More broadly still, Arnold's idealization of rural life, and his positive estimation of the 'peasant' virtues of spontaneity, naturalness, simplicity and humility reflected his participation in, or belated identification with, the Free German Youth Movement.

For Arnold, the earth was the principality of 'Anti-God', and was 'quite literally peopled . . . by death bringing spiritual beings'.[9] He believed that the actions of Anti-God and his demonic minions were manifested in all forms of violence, and in lust, deceit, greed and the institution of private property. The tragedy of the modern world was that man had become increasingly individualistic. Modern society was especially and essentially corrupt because it not only permitted, but glorified, individualism. Consequently, Arnold felt that all men living in modern societies were doomed to lead wretched lives – divorced from God and from true communion with their fellows.

The 'church-community' at Sannerz was modelled on the Primitive Church of Jerusalem, which Arnold believed was the fullest example of true Christian fellowship – of lives led in selfless attendance upon the promptings of the Spirit of God. From scriptural study, Arnold concluded that the lives of the early Christians, or at least of those who had given a 'true witness', were characterized by openness, communism, purity, pacifism, simplicity and unity.

Arnold insisted that at every moment of their lives his followers should strive to 'body-forth' these characteristics. True Christians should be charitable and hospitable, should share equally in all things and all labour, should be continent before marriage and faithful within it, should be non-violent, should not vote or hold public office, and should demonstrate humility and simplicity in their dress, manners, worship and artifacts. Above all, Arnold insisted that each member of the group should strive to subordinate his individual will to that of the Spirit of God, which in practice meant subordination to the will of Arnold, who was acknowledged as primary recipient of the promptings of the Spirit.

Finally, Arnold emphasized that the members of the Bruderhof were not committed simply to demonstrating the possibility of living lives of Christian fellowship, but also to 'winning back the garden' from Anti-God. Translating Arnold's metaphor, he rejected introversionism, and insisted that his followers had a duty to maintain and strengthen their society, and to evangelize. One quotation summarizes Arnold's utopian vision:

> This earth will become like one land, one garden where one righteousness and justice and one joy, one truth and one purity of mutual relationships, hold sway; so that only then shall joy really begin on this planet. This planet, the Earth, must be conquered for a new kingdom, for a new order, for a new unity, for a new joy.[10]

The group at Sannerz expanded rapidly to a total of about 50 people – full members, guests and children – in mid-1922, by which date the group was on the verge of financial collapse.[11] Arnold had intended that he and his followers should support themselves by agriculture, by craft-work and by publishing, but despite their identification with the peasantry, the predominantly urban middle-class sectarians were poor and unenthusiastic farmers.[12] Craft industries were only minimally developed, and the publishing house made little or no profit. At Sannerz, as indeed throughout most of the history of the group, the sectarians relied partially on gifts from sympathizers and remittances from disapproving relatives for the maintenance of their 'independent' existence.

In July of 1922, the collapse of the German mark led external supporters of the publishing house to withdraw their funds and, after a series of acrimonious meetings, some 40 people decided to leave the group. By October of 1922, only the Arnolds and a handful of loyal followers were left at Sannerz. This mass defection does not appear to have shaken Arnold's confidence in his mission. Publishing was resumed in 1923, and the group had again expanded to a total of about 45 by 1927, in which year pressure on accommodation prompted the sectarians to move away from Sannerz, and to establish the 'Rhön-bruderhof' on a dilapidated farm in the Rhön mountains.

In connection with the publication of a series of 'source books of Christian witness', Arnold had occasion to study some of the accounts and writings of the Hutterian Brethren and, in 1928, he was excited to discover that descendants of these pacifist Anabaptists were living in relatively prosperous communities in the United States and Canada. A complex mixture of financial and evangelical considerations prompted Arnold to correspond with the Hutterians, and in 1930 Arnold travelled to North America. After about a year spent journeying among the Hutterite communities, Arnold and his followers were accepted into the Hutterite Church. In December of 1930, at a Hutterian Bruderhof in Alberta, Arnold was ordained as 'Bishop' of the Hutterian Church in Germany.[13]

Arnold appears to have been disappointed by the Hutterians' sober response to his appeals for large sums of money, and many of his followers were dismayed by the extent of Hutterite 'legalism' – the requirement that both sexes should adopt Hutterian costume, and the prohibition of smoking, pictures, photographs and instrumental music. However, after Arnold's return to Germany, financial and disciplinary problems were eclipsed by the increasingly threatening political situation.

Hitler was elevated to the Chancellorship of the Reich in 1933, and, for once breaking with their principles, the sectarians participated in the plebiscite held in November of that year, and declared that they could only acknowledge and support a government appointed by God.[14] Shortly after this courageous action, the Rhönbruderhof was raided and searched by police and storm-troopers, and the group's school was closed on the grounds that insufficient patriotic instruction was provided. Early in 1934, the sectarians rented a hotel in Liechtenstein, and there established the 'Almbruderhof' as a refuge for their children, and for those young men who were liable for military service.

### Establishment in England and migration to Paraguay, 1935–41

The members of the Bruderhof were aware that the Almbruderhof was likely to provide only a temporary refuge and so, in the summer of 1935, Arnold and his eldest son Eberhard travelled to England to explore the possibility of establishing a community there, and to raise funds among sympathizers with whom the group had corresponded for several years.[15] On his return from England, Arnold entered a hospital in Darmstadt to undergo an operation to set a leg fracture. Complications developed and necessitated an amputation, but Arnold did not recover from this second operation, and he died on 22 November 1935.

Despite the tensions which had existed in the group since its incorporation in the Hutterite Church, after Arnold's death the majority of the members were united in their desire to escape from Nazi totalitarianism, and the threat of more severe persecution. In 1936, the group purchased a farm in England, at Ashton Keynes in Wiltshire. This 'Cotswold Bruderhof' was populated by English converts, and by the sectarians from the Rhönbruderhof, which was closed by the Gestapo in April 1937, and from the Liechtenstein Almbruderhof, which was closed in March of 1938. By the end of this latter year, the Cotswold Bruderhof had a total population of 210 people, 90 of whom were children.

The members of the sect who re-assembled at Ashton Keynes were convinced that their escape from Nazi persecution was providential and, fired by this demonstration of God's concern for his faithful servants, they enthusiastically embarked on recreating the church-community – the 'mustard seed' from which would grow the future world order. They were aided in this task by the fact that, as refugees from Germany, they received considerable sympathy from the general public and, initially, from their neighbours in Wiltshire. More concretely, they also received aid in cash and kind from interested individuals, and from a variety of pacifist groups, predominantly the Quakers.

The mixed arable and dairy farms purchased and rented at Ashton Keynes were fertile, and the sectarians' agricultural knowledge had increased greatly in a decade of labour on the exposed fields of the Rhönbruderhof. They were soon able to produce a surplus of wheat and dairy products, and by 1939 had established regular rounds for the sale of bread, eggs and milk in the neighbouring villages and in Swindon.

In the spring of 1939, pressure on accommodation at the Cotswold Bruderhof led the group to purchase a large house and farm some five miles from Ashton Keynes. Before the purchase, various local land-owners expressed opposition to the transaction and, presumably from anti-German sentiments, to any further expansion of the group.

Somewhat dismayed, but undeterred, the sectarians established the independent 'Oaksey Bruderhof'.

Craft industries, including the manufacture of such items as wooden bowls and ivory bookmarks, had been carried on in a desultory fashion in the Rhönbruderhof, and at Ashton Keynes such manufactures were founded on a larger scale and a more regular basis. With financial assistance from Quaker sympathizers a turnery was established, and a wide range of small wooden items was offered for sale. In all of their products the sectarians strove to give expression to the simplicity and disciplined harmony which was the fruit of their unceasing struggle to extirpate the 'cancer of individualism'.

In March of 1938, the sectarians began publication of a quarterly periodical, *The Plough*, subtitled, 'Towards the Coming Order'. In this journal, which was initially published in English and German editions, the sectarians provided accounts of the history of the sect in Germany, translations of Hutterian manuscripts and copious selections from the writings of Eberhard Arnold. In addition, the periodical contained news and notices relating to a variety of reformist and communitarian ventures, which ranged from secular anarchistic communes to the Quaker agricultural settlement among the unemployed at Brynmawr. In providing such a forum the members of the Bruderhof were following Eberhard Arnold's injunction that, in order to make converts, they should keep in touch with all partially enlightened 'movements of the times', while holding themselves aloof from the corrupting influence of worldly persons and causes.

Throughout this period, the members of the group continued to wear the sixteenth-century peasant costumes of the Hutterians, and to conform to most of the other Hutterian behavioural restrictions. While the sectarians regarded themselves as members of the Hutterian Church, this did not prevent them from hoping that the Hutterians could be won from their 'legalism', or from looking on the Hutterite communities as mission territories. In August of 1940, three missionaries were sent to evangelize among the Hutterians, and among a small group of Hungarians in Alberta who had expressed a wish to join the Bruderhof. Neither venture was successful, and the three grandly entitled 'witnesses to the west' eventually rejoined the group after its migration to Paraguay.

As a result of evangelistic activities in England in the period 1937 to 1939, some 40 English adults made a full commitment to the sect. The Bruderhof have always insisted that their message and style of

life appeals equally to all men, and in their publications have frequently stressed the social heterogeneity of the persons 'sent' to the
sect.[16] Despite this insistence, throughout the history of the group,
the majority of converts appear to have come from lower middle or
middle-class urban backgrounds. Several contributors to *The Plough*
wrote of the poverty which they had endured before joining the group,
but in most cases such poverty appears to have been accepted volun-
tarily, as a gesture of solidarity with the underprivileged, and of
renunciation of middle-class life-styles.[17]

At the time of their migration to England, the sectarians' status as
conscientious objectors was accorded official recognition by the
Home Secretary and, as already indicated, the group received a fair
amount of favourable publicity in national journals and newspapers.[18]
However, in the neighbourhood of Ashton Keynes, throughout 1938
and the early part of 1939, the threat of war and the accompanying
upsurge of militaristic and anti-German sentiments led to a steady
increase in hostility towards the sect.

After the outbreak of the Second World War, or, more accurately,
after the cessation of the 'phoney war', local hostility towards the
predominantly German-speaking sectarians greatly intensified. In
late May of 1940, the Swindon press reported that there was a sharp
division of opinion on the question of whether or not the German
members of the Bruderhof should be interned. Not content simply
with recording popular sentiments, the newspaper's commentator on
local affairs unequivocally supported internment on the 'common
sense' grounds that there might be Fifth Columnists among the
sectarians.[19]

In the same edition of *The Swindon Advertiser*, hostility to the
group was made respectable by the publication of the views of two
local dignitaries who supported internment – the vicar of Ashton
Keynes and, more importantly, the MP for Swindon, Mr W. Wakefield. The latter blatantly pandered to the majority opinion of his
constituents and, more specifically, to those tradesmen who claimed
that in view of the shortage of masculine labour, the Bruderhof
offered unfair economic competition in their bread and milk rounds.
In this connection, Mr Wakefield stated that he had no sympathy
with persons who 'pinched the business interests of men called to the
colours'. Brushing aside the remarks of a Bruderhof spokesman who
pointed out that the sectarians had left Germany precisely because
Hitler refused to recognize their pacifism, Mr Wakefield stated that

in his opinion the members of the Bruderhof were unchristian because they:

> . . . shelter behind their religious ideas and refuse to fight for the country that has given them shelter.[20]

A month later, *The Swindon Advertiser* reprinted a letter sent by a resident of Oaksey to the Home Secretary, in which it was stated that the whole district was unanimous in not wanting this 'alien community' in their midst, and which requested that all the members of the Bruderhof, German and British nationals alike, should be interned.[21]

Faced with unreasoning and intransigent hostility, with a local boycott of their delivery rounds, and with the Home Secretary's statement that he was unable to guarantee the German members freedom from internment for the duration of the war, the sectarians decided to leave England. Initially they planned to migrate to Canada, presumably in order to be in the vicinity of the most sympathetic Hutterian communities, but they were refused entry by the Canadian Government.

Eventually, after negotiations with the British Government, the sectarians received permission to emigrate to Paraguay, the only country which offered freedom of conscience, as well as abundant cheap land. In the first weeks of 1941, approximately 350 people sailed in six groups for Paraguay and, aided considerably by Mennonite settlers, re-assembled in eastern Paraguay on the 21,000 acre 'Primavera' estate which the group eventually purchased.

For the greater part of the next two decades, the majority of the sectarians lived in Paraguay where, after suffering considerably from an inadequate diet and from tropical diseases, they established three communities, and a hospital which extended its services freely to the neighbouring Indians. The geographic and cultural isolation of the Paraguayan communities was such as virtually to preclude successful evangelization but, by 1957, primarily as a result of natural increase, the total population of the Paraguayan communities had risen to some 700 people.[22]

### Re-establishment and expansion in England, 1942–58

When the sectarians migrated to Paraguay, three of the English members were left behind to complete the sale of the group's property at Ashton Keynes. While conducting negotiations for the sale, these three corresponded and visited with sympathizers and, by Christmas of 1941, the group had increased to a total of 19.

The British Government was reluctant to grant permission for the entire group to leave the country and, after correspondence with Primavera, it was decided to establish a new community in England. Accordingly, in March of 1942, a 180-acre farm was bought at Lower Bromdon, on the Clee Hills in Shropshire. The 'Wheathill Bruderhof' was formally established in December of 1942, by which date the group numbered 33.[23]

For the next few years the sectarians were primarily concerned to establish Wheathill on a sound economic basis. With some assistance from the Paraguayan group, and with capital brought in by converts, they were able to purchase several farms adjacent to Wheathill, and to improve their property considerably.[24] By 1949, they owned an estate of some 550 acres – mostly pasture. The sectarians' relations with their scattered neighbours appear to have been cordial and, after the end of the war, a number of German members returned from Paraguay in order to supplement the labour force, and to strengthen the convictions of the recent converts.

By the early 1950s, the communities in England and Paraguay were economically viable, and the sectarians had almost completely broken with the Hutterian Brethren.[25] Freed from constant concern with subsistence, and from the 'legalism' and introversionism which their connection with the Hutterians at least nominally implied, the Bruderhof once again turned enthusiastically to the world. To use the terminology currently employed by the sectarians, after the enforced period of 'creative withdrawal' in the 1940s, in the following decade they became concerned with 'outreach' – with demonstrating the superiority of their social arrangements to persons in the world.

The sectarians in Paraguay had little success in converting their Mennonite and Catholic Indian neighbours, but shortly after the end of the war they made contact with a number of communitarian groups in North America, and in 1952 sent several members on an exploratory tour of the eastern United States. These missionaries evoked considerable interest, and it was decided to establish a small community in North America. The 'Woodcrest Bruderhof' was founded in 1954, near Rifton in New York State, and subsequently two other communities were established, Oak Lake, Pennsylvania in 1957, and Evergreen, Connecticut, in 1958. Heinrich Arnold, the second son of Eberhard Arnold, was instrumental in the development of these three communities, and was acknowledged as the leader of the sectarians in North America.

For expedient as well as economic reasons the evangelistic activities of the English sectarians were drastically curtailed during the Second World War, but from 1943 the group at Wheathill circulated occasional newsletters to persons sympathetic to their way of life. By the end of 1945, as a result of the conversion of a handful of pacifists, the return of some members from Paraguay and natural increase, the population of Wheathill had grown to 90, and it reached a total of 200 by 1952.

The English sectarians' enthusiasm for renewed and extended contact with the world was evidenced in the spring of 1953 by the publication of a new quarterly series of *The Plough*, in the first edition of which the editors stated that their intention was to establish a 'vital contact with all seeking people'.[26]

The revived periodical was markedly less theological in content than its predecessor, and contained accounts of a wide range of groups whose ideals and goals to some degree approximated to those of the Bruderhof, as well as testimonies from converts, and reports of the development of the Bruderhof communities in North and South America. Some commentary on world affairs was provided, and such diverse international events as the Hungarian uprising and the Suez crisis were alike interpreted as 'signs of the times' which presaged the period when men would finally turn away from the corruption and violence of earthly governments and seek lives of peaceful, communistic fellowship.

The members of the Bruderhof did not confine themselves to literary evangelism but, throughout the 1950s, they sent groups of young people to speak publicly in Birmingham and other towns in the midlands. They also participated in a number of pacifist rallies and demonstrations (including the early Aldermaston marches), and in work camps and the meetings and conferences of a number of religious and political groups. In addition, several of the German members who had returned to Wheathill from Paraguay resumed correspondence with sympathizers on the Continent, and by Christmas of 1955 a small community, the 'Sinntalhof', was established in Germany, at Bad Brückenau, near Nuremburg.

The sectarians' evangelical fervour reached its height in 1956, and in this year a contributor to the group's periodical reported that in all the communities the members were struggling to develop a 'deepening sense of responsibility' for their 'world task' of evangelism.[27] Another contributor to the same edition of *The Plough* urged that the sectarians should learn Esperanto in order to facilitate international outreach.[28]

In November and December of 1956, delegates from all the communities met in Paraguay to discuss the future development of the sect, and the most efficient disposition of its resources. The persons attending this Interbruderhof Conference recognized that although the majority of the members lived in South America, greater opportunities for evangelism existed in Europe and North America. They therefore decided to run down the Paraguayan communities, and to transfer personnel and financial resources to these more promising areas.

More specifically, the delegates unanimously resolved that the major concentration of effort should be in the United States, that a new community should be established in the vicinity of a major English town, that future communities should be industrial rather than agricultural, that young persons should be encouraged to undertake higher education, and that a number of persons should be transferred immediately to Wheathill.

The decisions relating to the economic basis of future communities and to higher education reflected the success which had attended the North American sectarians' manufacture of wooden educational toys under the trademark 'Community Playthings'. The transfer of members to Wheathill was probably undertaken primarily in order to strengthen the faith of the more recent converts, some of whom appear to have been more interested in the political implications of communitarianism, rather than in the religious basis of 'the life'. As indicated, after 1953 the English sectarians developed a measure of *rapport* with such groups as the Fellowship of Reconciliation and the Campaign for Nuclear Disarmament, but occasional passages in the periodical emphasized the dangers of contamination by the world. Thus, in 1955, one writer stated flatly that

> the city on the hill may not lose its freedom and the essential character of its common life to any kingdom of this world, to any state or church or political party.[29]

A year after the Interbruderhof Conference, one of the farms at Wheathill was sold, and in 1958 the sectarians purchased Bulstrode Court, a large, dilapidated mansion with extensive grounds, at Gerrards Cross, on the fringe of London. The 'Bulstrode' community was established in the summer of 1958, and was populated by persons transferred from Wheathill, who maintained themselves by the manufacture of tubular steel farm gates and educational toys.

## Dissolution of the English communities, 1958–66

Eberhard Arnold insisted that any group which followed the clear and undivided promptings of the Spirit of God would be distinguished by the 'organic' unity of the thought and action of its members. During Arnold's lifetime, all important decisions were made unanimously by 'the Brotherhood', the assembly of the full members of the community, but Arnold's voice was dominant in that assembly. As in the sect today, any member who persisted in dissent after the 'leading of the Spirit' had become apparent to the majority was likely to be denounced for harbouring a 'bad spirit', and for endangering the fragile unity which bound the sectarians to God.

For fifteen years after Arnold's death in 1935, the sectarians were fully occupied with the arduous task of establishing their communities in England and Paraguay. Consequently, intra- and inter-community rivalries and tensions remained latent. However, once the sectarians turned to consider the practical implications of Arnold's injunction that they should 'conquer the earth' for God, a number of problems and conflicts developed.

All of the conflicts which arose in the 1950s appear to have stemmed from the sect's dual utopian commitment to withdrawal from the world and to evangelization. In each of the English and Paraguayan communities some members argued that to remain apart from the world would be to pervert Arnold's teachings, while others (probably the majority) insisted that, if the group were to 'maintain its light', it should shun all worldly interests and associations. In each community this ideological divergence generated a host of more specific policy questions, each of which could only be answered by tacit or actual resolution of the central dilemma.

The courses of action agreed upon at the 1956 Interbruderhof Conference exacerbated rather than resolved the conflicts which beset all but the recently established communities in the United States. Many of the sectarians regarded the proposed move to an industrial economy as a betrayal of Arnold's ideals, and many were loath to abandon the Paraguayan communities, which had been established at the cost of much hardship. In the Spring of 1959, a writer in *The Plough* acknowledged the existence of deep-rooted conflicts in the English groups, and appealed for

> . . . a spirit of brotherhood and co-operation not only within the communities, but between the communities . . .[30]

This appeal fell on deaf ears and, after 1959, the leaders of the English and Paraguayan groups were forced to admit their inability to attain internal unity. They sought a 'clear leading of the Spirit' and so turned to Heinrich Arnold, the leader of the three North American groups which at this period were relatively harmonious and were expanding rapidly.

The events of the years 1959 to 1962 are shrouded in secrecy, and the sectarians speak of this period with the greatest reluctance, but it appears that in his role as arbiter, Heinrich Arnold resolutely maintained that the cultivation of internal harmony and discipline was the primary task of the sectarians. He and his associates sought to 'purify' the group, and carried out successive purges of all those persons who had 'brought in a disturbance' by advocating closer alignment with the world.

Presumably, for many individuals secession appeared as the logical alternative to remaining in a sect which they believed had lost its vital spirit, but many others were expelled by the introversionist majority who clung to the sect as the storm-tossed, but divinely commissioned, 'ark' which alone could preserve them from worldly evil. In 1962, after the purges had ceased, the world population of the Bruderhof communities had fallen to half the 1958 total of 1,500.

The complete breakdown of agreement in the English communities can be dated with some precision from the fact that the sectarians summarily cancelled a conference of all 'friends of community' which they had called for Whitsun 1960, and that publication of *The Plough* ceased without notice after the spring issue of that year.

The contributors to the last issue of the periodical betrayed their introversionist leanings by roundly condemning the apathy and aimlessness of the British population and, somewhat contradictorily, by criticizing people who involved themselves with such organizations as War on Want and the Campaign for Nuclear Disarmament – both of which had earlier been endorsed by the Bruderhof. One contributor inveighed against the futility of piecemeal reform, and stated that, in view of the corruption of the world

... it must become clear, at least to those who call themselves Christian, that no amount of removing the fruits or pruning will alter the nature of the tree, nor the root from which it springs.[31]

By 1963, the sect's land at Wheathill had been sold and the community disbanded (as had the communities in Germany, Uruguay and Paraguay), and perhaps 120 people remained of the 1958 total of upwards of 250. A number of members who had left the sect were subsequently re-admitted to the Bulstrode community, which remained in existence until 1966. In this year, the Bulstrode estate and the English copyright on 'Community Playthings' were sold, and, 30 years after the group's arrival as refugees from Hitler's Germany, the last party of sectarians left England for the United States.

### Postscript

Some 200 people were re-admitted to the sect in the 'year of the harvest', 1963, increasing its numbers to about 900. Few converts have been made in recent years, and the population of the three American communities has increased only very slightly, despite a continuing high birth rate.

Heinrich Arnold was formally acknowledged as 'Bishop' or 'Vorsteher' of the sect in the mid-1960s, and in the last few years the group's introversionism has become steadily more pronounced. The world is condemned as a place of selfishness, greed, violence, and perhaps especially today, of sexual corruption. The present leaders of the Bruderhof communities, blessed with followers who have weathered the period of purge, appear to be almost entirely preoccupied with internal purification and the chimerical search for absolute unity.

The years in which the English and Paraguayan communities were established, and in which Bruderhof evangelism was most highly developed – the period 1935–65, from the death of Eberhard Arnold to the acknowledgment of his second son as supreme leader of the group – is now regarded as a time of apostasy; a time when the sectarians lacked the unity which they believe is at once the symptom and reward of selfless subordination to the Spirit of God.

### NOTES

1. Some of the research which underlies this article was made possible by a President's Research Grant from Simon Fraser University, British Columbia. I wish to express my gratitude for this award.

2. B. R. Wilson, 'An Analysis of Sect Development', *American Sociological Review*, Vol. 24, Feb. 1959, pp. 3–15, and 'Typologie des Sectes dans une Perspective Dynamique et Comparative', *Archives de Sociologie des Religions*, No. 16, July–Dec. 1963, pp. 49–63.

3. For such a discussion see John Whitworth, 'The Society of Brothers – A Contemporary Utopian Sect' (forthcoming).

4. Arnold's wife wrote an account of his life and of the vicissitudes of the sect in Germany. Emmy Arnold, *Torches Together. The Beginning and Early Years of the Bruderhof Communities*, The Plough Publishing House, Woodcrest, Rifton, NY 1964.

5. See Howard Becker, *German Youth: Bond or Free*, Kegan Paul, Trench, Trubner and Co. Ltd. 1946.

6. At the climax of this meeting the members pray silently while kneeling in a circle with palms upturned to symbolize their readiness to receive the Holy Spirit.

7. Howard Becker, op. cit., pp. 122–4, provides a description of this group.

8. Cited in the anonymous work *Eberhard Arnold. A Testimony of Church Community from his Life and Writings*, The Plough Publishing House, Woodcrest 1964, p. 5.

9. Eberhard Arnold, *When the Time Was Fulfilled – Advent and Christmas*, The Plough Publishing House, Woodcrest 1965, p. 121.

10. Eberhard Arnold, *God and Anti-God*, The Plough Publishing House, Ashton Keynes, Wilts 1939, p. 27.

11. Birth control is frowned upon, and large families have always been the norm in the Bruderhof. Consequently, at most periods in the group's history, almost half the total population of the sect has been under twenty-one years of age.

12. The person in charge of farming at Sannerz wanted to allow the group's neighbours to remove a dung-heap from the farmyard as it was an eye-sore. Emmy Arnold, op. cit., p. 66.

13. See Victor Peters, *All Things Common. The Hutterian Way of Life*, The University of Minnesota Press, Minneapolis 1965. The 'Schmiedenleut' group approached by Arnold remains the most liberal branch of the Hutterian Brethren, but liberalism is relative, and it says much for Arnold's persuasiveness that he was able to convince some of the Hutterians of his inspiration, and to extract some funds from the cautious sectarians.

14. They did this by gumming a statement of their views on to their ballot slips.

15. English Quakers provided considerable assistance for the sectarians in Liechtenstein, see *The Friend*, Vol. 93, No. 51, 20 December 1935, p. 1193.

16. See *The Plough*, Vol. 3, No. 2, Summer 1940, p. 56.

17. The author of a newsletter circulated by the sectarians in Paraguay mentioned that some of the English members had been 'tramp preachers' and had endured voluntary poverty in the slums of London. Cited in *Co-operative Living*, Vol. 5, No. 1, Fall 1953, p. 6.

18. See for example *The Spectator*, 11 June 1937, pp. 1087–8, and *Illustrated*, Vol. 1, No. 7, 15 April 1939, pp. 11–16.

19. *The Swindon Advertiser*, 31 May 1940, p. 1.

20. Loc. cit.

21. Ibid., 28 June 1940, p. 1.

22. The early struggles of the sectarians in Paraguay are described in a pamphlet by Sidney and Marjorie Hindley, *Work and Life at the Bruderhöfe in Paraguay*, The Society of Brothers, Wheathill Bruderhof, Bromdon, Shrops. 1943.

23. A description of this community is provided by W. H. G. Armytage, 'The Wheathill Bruderhof, 1942–58', *American Journal of Economics and Sociology*, Vol. 18, No. 3, April 1959, pp. 285–94.

24. At baptism every individual dedicates his property irrevocably to the sect.

25. The break came after 1950, when several Hutterites visited Paraguay, and were shocked to find the sectarians engaged in folk-dancing, play-acting and similar iniquitous practices.

26. *The Plough* (New Series), Vol. 1, No. 1, Spring 1953, p. 1.

27. Ibid., Vol. 4, No. 2, Summer 1956, p. 59.

28. Ibid., pp. 51–2.

29. Ibid., Vol. 3, No. 4, Winter 1955, p. 101.

30. *The Plough* (Second New Series), Vol. 2, No. 1, Spring 1959, p. 10.

31. Ibid., Vol. 3, No. 1, Spring 1960, p. 8.

# 7 John Wesley and the Origin and Decline of Ascetic Devotion

## Michael Hill and Bryan Turner

MAX WEBER is probably best known for his study of the relationship between Calvinistic Protestantism and the rise of Western rational capitalism. Whilst the debate – often narrowly historical, often niggling – which has surrounded this analysis of some of the features of Protestantism is certainly of critical importance, it has often obscured other, equally important aspects of Weber's general sociology. The adaptation of Calvinism to entrepreneurship was one case of a general phenomenon in the interaction of religion and society which Weber called 'routinization'. In this paper, Weber's concepts of legitimate authority, charisma, 'virtuoso religion' and the process of 'elective affinity' will be employed to study the Wesleyan devotional tradition in England. We will study its emergence from one of the Anglican traditions which can be distinguished after the Reformation and its development from the 'Holy Club' to the present day. This is clearly a very wide undertaking, and we can only hope to outline a general framework within which historical trends can be conceptualized.

It will be useful to start our discussion by considering the distinction which Weber makes between salvation religions and legalistic religions. Whereas salvation religions, in orienting the believer to his personal sanctification, are to some extent in conflict with the world, legalistic religions, which depend on the sacredness of law, are accommodated to the world. Salvation religions, however, frequently move towards traditional-legal acceptance of the world because their original fervour becomes routinized and systematized.[1] Routinization and the associated loss of pristine fervour and commitment can be curtailed by the charismatic breakthrough of the prophet. Typical of such breakthroughs are the activities of the Hebrew prophets. The charismatic leader, in revitalizing the religious life of the community, establishes a new basis of religious authority which brings him into conflict with the religious and secular authorities of the day.[2]

Weber's theory of charismatic breakthrough does not, however, commit Weber or Weberian sociologists to a 'Great Man' theory of history. Perhaps the most significant statement which Weber made about charisma is '(charisma) may be said to exist only in the process of originating'.[3] The point he is concerned to make is that the new loyalties demanded by a charismatic leader rarely correspond to already existing and articulate 'interests' among those groups which accept his authority. Such a conception of authority can be termed a materialistic Marxist interpretation, and it is interesting to note that the recent work of a contemporary Marxist makes precisely this assumption.[4] To Weber, an 'idea' in its inception rarely corresponds to previously conscious material interests. However, this concept is inseparable from that of 'routinization', by means of which Weber tempers the notion of new ideas and new loyalties. He posits a dynamic process which eventually brings his theory very close to that of the Marxists in that, once the charismatic message is adopted by the members of social groups and strata who choose to become followers (or more typically, 'disciples'), then it will be systematized and modified by these followers in the light of their own material needs. It is this interaction between the pristine message and the material demands of those who adopt the leader which is the central concern of Weber, and to which he gave the name routinization. Weber further believed that ideas were ultimately discredited in the face of history unless they corresponded to interests derived from the material basis of society. We can perhaps summarize his perspective by quoting the following epithet of Gerth and Mills:

Not Julius Caesar, but Caesarism: not Calvin, but Calvinism is Weber's concern.[5]

The two most important components of the concept of routinization are institutionalization and elective affinity. We can see the relevance of institutionalization if we note that, of the three types of authority – traditional, charismatic and legal-rational – which Weber analyses, charismatic authority is the most unstable since it depends on the personal heroism of the leader and on the enthusiastic support of his followers. The charismatic leader's death in particular poses basic problems for the continuity of the charismatic movement. As a result, the originally personal charisma becomes routinized as 'charisma of office' which, in a religious movement, typically takes the form of a priestly hierarchy or at least a formally differentiated hierarchy of religious professionals. The joyous festivals of the gathered followers become the formalized rituals of the church, which are administered by these professionals. The 'good news' of the charismatic breakthrough becomes the domain of specialists, who systematize the message into a theological system.

In addition to the institutionalization of the original group of leader and followers and the systematization of the message, there also occurs a process of selection from the core of the message of those elements which are particularly relevant to the group of individuals which has joined the movement; and at the same time additional elements are added to it: this is what Weber calls elective affinity. Instead of a close correlation between the leader's and his subsequent followers' interests, we may expect that the charismatic message will be interpreted in such a way that elements of it are sifted, selected out and supplemented to meet the material requirements of the new recruits. The process of election by convergence received its classic analysis in Weber's *The Protestant Ethic and the Spirit of Capitalism*.[6] The crux of his argument – one that is frequently misinterpreted – is *not* that Calvin or any of the other Protestant Reformers sanctioned capitalistic practice or that Calvinism 'caused' capitalism.[7] All he states was that there was an affinity – or correlation – between Calvinism and modern rational, as opposed to premodern capitalism;[8] and further, that the affinity arose as the result of a selection process which produced both a drive towards and a legitimation of economic activities which led to the rise of modern industry. In particular, the legitimation of a 'calling' in the sense of a worldly vocation was highly important. It is vital to stress that elective affinity is not intended to describe the permissive rationalization of questionable activities but rather the spontaneous and gradual convergence of a religious ethic and a materialistic spirit to produce a powerful motivation towards rational involvement in economic activities.[9]

We have noted that charismatic authority is the most unstable of Weber's three types, but this is not to state that radical change is a feature characteristic only of charismatic intervention. In this paper we hope to demonstrate the significance of traditional authority in this context.[10] Weber's concept of traditional authority contains the basic ideas of stability and continuity. Traditional authority is based on the performance of actions because they have always been performed and the occupation of positions of authority on a hereditary basis. Thus all the activities of the legitimate authorities in such a society must be evaluated by reference to established practice, whether the origins of the practice are based on myth or on fact. However, Weber makes it quite clear that radical innovatory actions can be legitimately performed by any group which claims to be *restating* some traditional practice which the existing authorities have either abused or abandoned. This is what we will label a 'revolution by tradition' and its implications will be pointed out. It is, in effect, the Weberian version of a 'Golden Age' theory, whereby a group or an individual in a traditional authority structure reiterates the original basis of legitimacy in order to compare unfavourably the present incumbents of authority positions.

On the basis of this outline of Weberian theory we will analyse two major aspects of Methodist history. Firstly, we will construct a model of Weber's category of traditional authority as applied to the Church of England in order to place in sociological perspective the various 'parties' in the church and their relevance for the origins of Methodism. As part of this discussion we will try to suggest some of the basic similarities between the Wesleyan and Tractarian revivals. The second part of the paper will concentrate on the modifications of 'ascetic devotionalism' in the Wesleyan and, at a later stage, Methodist Church. It will outline the typical elements of Wesley's devotionalism, as a criterion for establishing the sort of 'elections' which were made from the original concept of holiness by the social groups which were recruited to Wesleyanism. We will conclude this section by taking two contemporary surveys of Methodist devotion[11] which mark, as it were, the final stages of divergence from the original devotional norm.

Of prime importance for the first stage of our argument is the *mixed tradition* of Anglicanism: by this we mean that within the Church of England there are distinct groups which regard different periods in the church's history as crucial, and these groups are usually referred to as schools of 'churchmanship'. There have been in fact four main referents of tradition to which groups within the Church of England could resort in claims of legitimacy. Firstly, there was the notion of an important tradition stemming from the Reformation. Some Anglicans saw their church quite explicitly as part of a wider continental Protestant tradition, and several attempts were made in the eighteenth century to achieve unity of some sort with continental Protestant bodies. One of these schemes involved the bestowal of a valid apostolic episcopal succession on the Lutheran Church. The Erastians had a particularly strong notion of a Reformation tradition, and among this group were a number of low church Whigs who were prepared to go a long way in compromising with the Dissenters in an attempt to form a *national* church.

The second traditional referent was the Middle Ages, though this was only to gain importance in claims to legitimacy in the nineteenth century. The later Anglo-Catholics looked to the mediaeval Church of England – which they called the *Ecclesia Anglicana* – as the basis of their pre-Reformation tradition. Allchin expresses this neatly:

> The Tractarians, in their desire to assert the continuity of the post-Reformation Church of England with the mediaeval Church, possibly overestimated this debt.[12]

Coupled with Gothic romanticism, this tradition finds its *reductio ad absurdum* in Father Ignatius of Llanthony. During the eighteenth century, however, the Middle Ages tradition was generally devalued, particularly as represented in Gothic architecture: in fact, the white-washing of church interiors had an ideological as well as an aesthetic justification. The Age of Reason had no particular use for traditional legitimations derived from what was generally seen as an age of superstition.

The third traditional referent was the church of the gospels and the Acts of the Apostles. The Protestant wing of the Church of England saw the Reformation as a return to this pristine state following a period of decline in Western Catholicism during the Middle Ages. Latourette gives an excellent summary of this variant:

> Their distinctive convictions, Protestants declared, were of the essence of the Gospel and therefore were not new. They insisted that theirs was the primitive and therefore the true Christianity and that it was not they, but the Roman Catholics who were innovators and heretics.[13]

This is a very obvious 'revolution by tradition', and we term this the Protestant 'step' theory of church history to contrast it with the Catholic continuity theory.[14] From the Protestant viewpoint the bible is the sole source of authority, so for this group the model of pristine purity is the New Testament church. Perhaps the most clear statement of this traditional referent of legitimacy in the eighteenth century is given by Richard Watson, Regius Professor of Divinity at Cambridge:

I reduced the study of divinity into as narrow a compass as I could, for I determined to study nothing but my Bible, being much unconcerned about the opinions of councils, fathers, churches, bishops and other men as little inspired as myself . . .[15]

It might be argued against our elaboration of the New Testament church as a distinct traditional referent that it is only a particular example of our first category, the Reformation tradition, and that all Christian groups base their organization more or less on the New Testament. Nevertheless, we would maintain that it is useful to distinguish a scriptural tradition since acceptance of the Reformation then becomes largely *conditional* on the extent to which the latter can be interpreted as a reinstatement of the primary tradition. Thus the Trinitarian controversy of the eighteenth century could be evinced as one instance of the scriptural tradition asserting itself over the major Reformation tradition. By this we mean that, while the main Protestant groups formed at the time of the Reformation had accepted the doctrine of the Trinity elaborated during the post-gospel church, it was still open for Protestant groups to reinterpret this doctrine in a more radical way by reference direct to the New Testament. In this case the Reformation tradition becomes secondary to an interpretation of the New Testament tradition. As a documentary premise for all Christian traditions the latter is by no means uncontroversial, and interpretations of it frequently make use of the external evidence of certain periods of church history, but statements like that of Richard Watson (noted above) suggest that we should view this as a distinct source of tradition.

Finally, the traditional referent with which we are most concerned is that of the primitive church. It was, we believe, the tradition on which both early Methodism and the early Tractarian movement legitimated their innovations. This tradition contained not only a notion of the scriptural basis of Christian organization but also of the church of the first four or five councils. Reference to this tradition has always been important for 'enthusiasts', as Knox rightly points out, but when he states so forcibly that the first few centuries of Christianity did not conform to the realities of pristine purity in the way sectarians imagined, Knox cuts the ground from under his own feet, because the primitive church is an important part of the Catholic 'continuum' of church history.[16] In the Church of England, we can trace the traditional referent of the primitive church as far back as its sixteenth century origins. The Homilies were one of the earliest

statements of Anglican theological opinion, and of these Lowther
Clarke says:

> ... the double method of proof, from the Bible and the Fathers, is characteristic
> of nearly all the Homilies.[17]

The high church party was the most consistent bearer of this tradition
– represented notably in the early seventeenth century by Laud – and
by the end of the seventeenth century the tradition was very much
associated with this party and with the Nonjurors in particular. However, at the end of the seventeenth and the beginning of the eighteenth
centuries this tradition was very much weakened, partly due to the
departure of the Nonjurors and the preferment of low church Whig
bishops, and partly as a result of the substitutions of reason in place
of antiquity as the source of doctrinal authority. There appears to be
general agreement that in the period immediately before the Methodist revival the main features of established Christianity can be listed
as Erastian, rationalistic, individualistic and dominated by a strong
belief in the interconnexion of church and state.

Against this background it is not difficult to place John Wesley's
initial innovations very firmly in the high church tradition which
emphasized the importance of the primitive church: indeed, the label
'innovations' is only appropriate in the context of the eighteenth century Church of England because in most cases the practices which
Wesley instituted were simply reinstatements of primitive practices.
It is in this sense that we are using the concept of a radical change
within traditional authority, and we are locating the particular tradition within the mixed tradition of the Church of England. An extended quotation from Balleine will illustrate the source of legitimacy
for Wesley's organizational innovations:

> Probably most earnest men, who take an interest in theology, pass through a
> stage in which they feel strongly the glamour of Antiquity. They construct for
> themselves a picture of the Past vague and highly idealized, and then long to
> restore once more the Golden Age that has gone. This was the state of mind of
> the Methodists in 1732. ... The following memorandum by John Wesley shows
> how far this impulse was carrying them: 'I believe it is a duty to observe so far
> as I can (1) to baptise by immersion; (2) to use Water, Oblation of Elements,
> Invocation, Alms, a Prothesis, in the Eucharist; (3) to pray for the faithful de-
> parted; (4) to pray standing on Sunday in Pentecost; (5) to abstain from blood
> and things strangled.' It was only a passing phase, but it left its mark. To the
> end of his life Wesley was a Patristic student; he translated the Apostolic
> Fathers for the use of his preachers; and most of the things that were considered
> innovations in the societies that he organized later – the class-meetings, the
> love-feasts, the quarterly ticket, the day-break services, the watch-nights, the

separate seats for men and women – were really revivals of customs of the Primitive Church.[18]

We would argue that the affinity between the Wesleyan and Tractarian movements which was noted by several high church Anglicans in the nineteenth century and by more recent writers[19] resulted from the restatement which both movements made of the primitive church tradition. It is certainly not true to state, as Skevington Wood does, that the Oxford Movement depreciated the Evangelical Movement.[20] Indeed some of the most prominent members of the Oxford Movement saw a strong resemblance between the Wesleyan revival and their own, and they frequently expressed regret that the Church of England had shown so little understanding of the Methodists.[21] An important question thus arises: why, if the Methodist and Tractarian revivals had certain common features, did they have such profoundly different results? Much of the second half of this paper will be concerned with the development of Methodism away from its Anglican base, but a few preliminary observations can be made at this point. In many ways, the basic reason behind both revivals was the necessity to respecify the spiritual autonomy of the Church of England in periods when it was being subjected to State incursions: we have already set the background of the Methodist revival, and it will be remembered that the Oxford Movement of 1833 began partly in response to the suppression by Parliament of ten Irish bishoprics. Clearly, the primitive church was a powerful traditional referent in stressing this autonomy. But the comparison could be made in two different ways. Either the primitive church could be seen as the point of origin of the routinized charismatic roles in the contemporary church – thus crystallizing the contemporary organization into a set of formal and autonomous offices[22] – or it could be seen as legitimating the sort of personal charismatic activity which ultimately overflowed the formal roles of the organization: a particularly good example of this is field-preaching. The Tractarians took the first alternative and the Methodists the second. John Wesley himself had few doubts about the fluidity of the primitive church's organization, as is amply demonstrated by his statement at the fourth Annual Conference of 1747 that there was no thought of uniformity in the government of all the churches until the time of Constantine, and that there would not have been uniformity then if men had only consulted the will of God.[23] At the same time, Wesley cannot altogether be called a charismatic leader (though he does have certain charismatic qualities) because he was primarily concerned to revive existing, albeit neglected obligations rather than to establish new obligations: to supplement rather than to supplant. It was simply that the model of church organization which he derived from the high church tradition of the Church of England was more capable of charismatic reinterpretation in his version than was the Tractarian model.

We would argue that Wesley conforms most closely to Weber's concept of the 'religious virtuoso'.[24] Despite some elements of charisma, Wesley did not intentionally and explicitly attempt to break with established religion or with society as such. Rather he sought to reintensify devotional life, which would in turn provide the religious basis for disciplined engagement in the world. To establish this point, namely that pristine Wesleyanism was a systematization and intensification of the path to personal sanctification, we will examine briefly the institutions which Wesley established and the rules of life which were fostered in these institutions.

Much can be learned from the epithets which were attached to the group of Oxford students of Wesley's university days. 'Methodists', 'Bible Moths' and 'Holy Club' all point to the adherence of the Wesleys and their associates to virtuoso religion. Wesley accepted the title 'methodist' as 'one who lives according to the method laid down in the bible'.[25] The Oxford 'method' included daily observation of the offices, fasting, penance and mortification: the parallel with some of the early Tractarians is quite striking. Wesley's attraction, as we have noted, was originally towards aspects of specifically Catholic method, and it was only after the Oxford and Georgia period that his asceticism took a predominantly Puritan bent. In Weber's typology of ascetic activity, asceticism can take two major forms – world abnegation (*weltablehrende*) or world mastery (*innerweltliche*). The Catholic form of asceticism is typically seen as rejecting the world and concentrating on other-worldly goals, while Puritan asceticism is practised in the world and is directed towards a radical transformation of the world by this-worldly means. It is worth noting that in no Christian group does either type of asceticism occur exclusively: even the most contemplative religious order will incorporate some form of manual or parish work into its practices, for example. The importance of this distinction, as in all ideal types, lies in its *emphasis*. Thus, although the early Methodists were engaged in various forms of social work – the Oxford Methodists, for instance, pleased their bishop by visiting prisoners in the castle – this may be regarded as secondary to their world-rejecting asceticism which they based on the model of the primitive church. It was in the later stage of Methodism that asceticism became predominantly of the type Weber called world-mastery.

Whilst the Holy Club to some extent formed the basic model for the growth of Methodism, refinements and additions were developed as a result of Wesley's association with the Moravians.[26] The method of the virtuoso life is summed up in Wesley's treatment of instituted and prudential means of grace.[27] The instituted means are:

Prayer (private, family, public);
Searching the scriptures (by reading, meditating, hearing);
The Lord's Supper;
Fasting;
Christian Conference;

Prudential means, largely adopted from Moravian practice, include:

Meeting with the band, and the class.

Prudential means in particular reveal the nature of Wesleyan virtuoso religiousness. Bands were composed of the most devout members, who met for mutual examination on a weekly basis.[28] Bands, thus, reflected the discipline of penance which Wesley had established at Oxford. At a later date, it became the custom to divide the whole society into classes, which provided for both devotion and oversight. Early Wesleyanism, therefore, was stratified into a merit-order, which was based on the criterion of religious virtue. At the apex of the system were Wesley and the assistants, followed by the leaders of bands and classes and at the bottom, the undifferentiated members. The society itself was seen as an order within the Church of England of the more earnest followers of the 'method'.[29] The activities of the Methodist society were thus additions and intensifications of the pattern of religious life which was provided by the established church. The Methodist society in eighteenth-century Anglicanism represented an 'aristocratic' form of the religious life based on virtuoso living:

It follows from all this that all intensive religiosity has a tendency towards a sort of social stratification, in accordance with differences in the charismatic qualifications. 'Heroic' or 'virtuoso' religiosity is opposed to mass religiosity. By 'mass' we understand those who are religiously 'unmusical'; we do not, of course, mean those who occupy an inferior position in the secular order.[30]

Having put forward our claim that Wesleyan devotion conforms to religious virtuoso activity, we turn now to the elections from the core tradition by those who subsequently became Wesleyans. The key to the elective process in Wesleyanism is to be found in the strain which emerged between the aristocratic elements of virtuoso religion and Wesleyan commitment to Arminianism. The purity of practice could have been maintained to some extent on the basis of elitist election to the society: Bryan Wilson, for instance, has shown how the criteria of entry may serve as a means of sect-maintenance. Arminianism, however, led in the opposite direction, that is, to mass religion. Whilst it is clear from the journals that Wesley recruited considerable numbers from the deprived sections of English society, there can be little doubt that by the end of the eighteenth century the Methodist local leadership was drawn from small manufacturers and traders. Such groups had a natural affinity with what might be termed Wesley's ethical asceticism, rejection of luxury, self-discipline, family duty, in short the calling in the world. The sifting of the ethical and ecclesiastical component is succinctly expressed by John Lawson:

> Busy shop-keepers approved of that part of the Methodist discipline which in the name of God bade them 'scorn delights and live laborious days'. They had room for regular Sunday service and dutiful family prayers. However, the more ascetic and ecclesiastical discipline of the 'morning preaching', the Friday fast, and having one's heart searched to the bottom, at the penitential Band was less congenial.[31]

The transition from virtuoso religion to mass religion was painfully obvious to Wesley himself:

> For the Methodists in every place grow diligent and frugal; consequently they increase in goods. Hence they proportionately increase in pride, in anger, in the desire of the flesh, the desire of the eyes, and the pride of life. So, although the form of religion remains, the spirit is swiftly vanishing away.[32]

The decline of ascetic devotionalism, which started in Wesley's own lifetime, was reinforced in the middle and late nineteenth century by the continual pull towards a congregational polity, in which the minister was simply a representative of the congregation, away from the Wesleyan connexional polity.[33] An important indicator of these institutional and social changes within Methodism in the nineteenth century is offered by the changes in the Methodist class system. Mutual examination became tedious to the liberal, middle-class Methodists and, as Currie notes,

> By the end of the nineteenth century, members could absent themselves from class with impunity, not least because their absence would scarcely be noticed.[34]

Changing attitudes towards the class meeting are reflected in the increasing size of the Methodist class.[35] Because of these increases in the size of the classes, it would appear that such classes have ceased to meet in groups. Of the 57 churches which were sampled in a recent survey of Yorkshire Methodists, only two had classes which met regularly. The modern class system was described by one minister in the area as a 'ticket system', that is, members receive class tickets and may be visited by their class leader but they rarely meet in groups as such. Classes in Methodism, even where they do meet, have ceased to fulfil those essential ascetic and devotional functions for which they were originally created.

During the nineteenth century, the virtuoso core of the Wesleyan devotional tradition had been gradually modified, whittled away and sieved to meet the needs of the middle-class Methodists, who were engaged in secular occupations which conflicted with the ecclesiastical discipline of the Wesleys. By the end of the century, Wesleyan worship became increasingly identical with other nonconformist traditions in which the Sunday sermon and, where it survived, family prayer, was the acme of the week's devotional exercise. In fact, the sermon in the Sunday service was the only religious activity for many Methodists. However, the virtuoso core of the tradition was never entirely swamped and attempts were made to revive the ascetic tradition by the Methodist Sacramental Fellowship in 1935. The aims of the MSF were three-fold: to re-affirm the faith that inspired the Evangelical revival, to make the communion service central to the life of the Methodist Church and to work for reunion (principally with the Anglican Church). Members of the MSF followed a simple rule of religious life, namely daily prayer, daily scripture reading and a minimum monthly reception of Holy Communion. J. E. Rattenbury, one of the founder members of MSF, expressed the disquiet felt by those following a virtuoso religious style for the 'growing irreverence of our services' and noted amongst other things: the constant chattering in the House of the Lord, the sitting posture at prayer and utter disrespect for sacred objects such as the Communion Table.[36] Considerable opposition to the aims of the MSF arose among Methodists who now espoused a non-virtuoso style of religious activity. In 1937, Conference received thirteen memorials from circuits and one from a Synod asking for an investigation of the principles of the MSF. Despite early opposition, the mood of the Methodist Church has changed considerably. Methodist architecture and Methodist worship has been greatly influenced by, amongst other things, the ecumenical movement and the associated revival of interest in liturgy. The question which remains, and which we will attempt to answer, is: has the renewal of interest in virtuoso religion greatly influenced the mass religious style of the Methodist laity?

In our discussion of contemporary religious practice we find it convenient to distinguish between two related types of practice. These we will call ritual and devotional practice. The first is essentially formal and public, while the second is informal and normally private.[37]

### Ritual

The most elementary and typical form of public ritual is, of course, attendance at Sunday worship. For Wesley and for the early Wesleyans, observance of the Sabbath was an essential part of the week's religious activities. The band rules of 1744 established the norm:

> Constantly to attend on all the ordinances of God; in particular, 1. To be at Church and at the Lord's Table every week.[38]

To a large extent, contemporary Methodists faithfully follow this injunction of weekly attendance at church. Among members of the Methodist Church in a Yorkshire District in 1968 for example, 74% attended regularly each week and 14% attended at least once a month. Similar figures for a sample of Methodists in the London area in 1967 showed that 70% attended on average once a week and 21% attended on average once a month. However, 'To be at church' in eighteenth-century Wesleyanism meant both attendance at the Anglican church and attendance at the Methodist preaching house. The devout Methodist of the 1750s would hear a Methodist sermon at five in the morning, attend his parish church at the morning service and again in the afternoon for the evening service. Finally, at five in the afternoon he would hear another sermon in the Methodist preaching house. The modern Methodist pattern is very different. Apart from the separation of the Anglican and Methodist Churches and the alteration of times of service, contemporary Methodists typically attend only one service, morning or evening, on Sunday. Over half (62%) of the Yorkshire Methodists went to only one service on a Sunday: just over a third (36%) went to both. It seems evident that the disciplined, virtuoso style of Sunday worship in early Wesleyanism has been replaced by a mass religious style in which, for many Methodists, Sunday worship is not seen as a demanding activity. Pickering has indicated the increasing importance of a 'leisure ethos', especially within nonconformity and in particular Methodism.[39]

We have already noted that Methodists ceased to avail themselves of the Lord's Supper at 'every opportunity'.[40] By the beginning of the twentieth century, eucharistic devotion had been undermined as a central part of Methodist worship. Attempts were made to re-emphasize this aspect of corporate worship by the MSF and in 1947 Conference laid down monthly communion as a minimum requirement. While monthly communion does not match early Wesleyan practice, it does represent a stiffening of ascetic devotion. This is partly reflected in the frequency of communion of the Methodists in the two surveys. Half of the members of the Yorkshire churches received communion monthly, as against 62% of the London group; 25% of the Yorkshire Methodists attended every three months, but 19% still received communion once a year or less. 32% of the London group attended less than once a month but occasionally.

The discipline of the ritual life has evidently declined from the standard which Wesley set for himself and his followers. Despite the renewal of interest in eucharistic worship, a return to virtuoso religion appears difficult to achieve. However, ritual is only one type of religious practice, and it may be that the devotional type of practice – private, 'closet' religion – is more congenial to the ethos of Wesleyanism. This view has been put forward by A. R. George, who claims that in Methodism

> Spontaneity is preferred to artificiality; there is a healthy fear of merely formal religion.[41]

It is necessary, therefore, in assessing changes within Wesleyan devotionalism, to turn to private and informal patterns of practice.

## Devotion

A basic component of private practice is, of course, prayer. Most contemporary Methodists feel that prayer is essential, but there is some difference between their valuation and their actual practice. While 89% of the Yorkshire Methodists said that prayer was extremely or fairly important in their lives, only 46% prayed regularly – once a day or more – and 17% said they never or hardly ever prayed.

It may be argued that, in emphasizing the ascetic forms of Wesleyan devotion, we have overemphasized the Catholic strain in Wesley's synthesis of Catholic and Puritan traditions. Although this position may be defensible in terms of our concentration on eucharistic ritual, there can be no doubt that the regular 'searching of the scripture' is

characteristic of Puritan and Wesleyan devotion. Regular bible reading, therefore, will be a strong indicator of disciplined, Puritan devotion: it is here that the vast majority of contemporary Methodists
diverge. Only 12% of the Yorkshire Methodists read their bible daily,
and 45% seldom or never read the bible. The majority are 'irregular
bible readers'. It seems, then, that in addition to a decline in the
Catholic element of Wesleyan ascetic devotion there has been a parallel diminution of its Puritan aspects.

Just as our attention to the ascetic disciplines of Wesleyan worship
needs to be examined in terms of both Catholic and Puritan emphases,
so the solemn, austere Puritan note requires the balance of what is
often regarded as the corner-stone of Methodist worship, namely the
fellowship which is enjoyed by the company of the faithful. Although
holiness is the central emphasis of Wesleyanism, this holiness was not
individualistic, but was set within the context of the fellowship of believers. Wesley understood the primitive church tradition as one in
which the faithful were gathered together in mutual help and friendship. Wesley criticized the established church, whose parishioners he
described as 'a rope of sand', for failing to provide for Christian
fellowship. The prudential means of grace had, consequently, the
double function of providing discipline and fellowship. The fellowship of believers was buttressed by kinship relations and in Methodism 'fellowship' and 'family religion' are used interchangeably. Much
of the emphasis on fellowship still survives in local house-meetings
and in university Methsoc groups. The evidence of extensive friendship within Methodism suggests that the common reference to 'fellowship' is more than mere lip-service to a dead tradition. Data from the
Leeds survey go some way in confirming that in many ways the
Methodist society is a community rather than an audience. 21% of
the sample had all of their five best friends in their congregation, and
23% had three to four of their best friends. Similarly, in the London
survey, when respondents were asked to write their own comments
on the Methodist Church many of them described its 'fellowship'. On
the other hand, it is difficult to provide any satisfactory measure of
the concept of 'fellowship', and frequency of friendship tells us little
of its content. There is, in short, a vast difference between superficial
'chumminess' and the more intensive euphoria of the religious community. Where the tradition breaks down is that the original bands
and classes provided both discipline and fellowship. The religious
orders' ethos[42] of watchfulness and oversight has disappeared with

the abandonment of the bands, watch-nights and love-feasts and the change in the nature and function of classes. Finally, much of the pristine fellowship of Methodism was based on the fact of conversion, and on mutual growth in holiness. Today's fellowship depends more heavily on family background and residence.

## Conclusion

In this paper we have argued that, in its pristine form, the religious style of John Wesley is best understood as virtuoso religious activity. The discipline of his own life and that which was accepted by the Holy Club at Oxford and by the early Wesleyan 'helpers' involved a systematization and intensification of the religious life. By a synthesis of primitive church practice, continental devotionalism and Puritan asceticism, Wesley laid the foundations of a virtuoso religious movement. For Wesley, however, heroic religion became less identified with contemplative or mystical religiosity and involved activity in the world. World-mastery in Wesleyanism took the form of, on the one hand, intense social activity and, on the other, of evangelism.

Recruits to Wesleyanism found their secular life-style, particularly a trading-commercial life-style, to be incompatible with the Wesley's ascetic, ecclesiastical discipline. Middle-class Methodists, we have argued, had an affinity with Wesley's ethical rather than ecclesiastical virtuosity. The consequent election from the original Wesleyan model brought Methodism closer to mass religious rather than virtuoso religious styles.

Contemporary practice, ritual and devotion exhibit a more relaxed, less demanding religious style – more appropriate to the 'leisure ethos' of religion[43] – than that established by Wesley. Whilst the ascetic religious life in Wesleyanism and modern Methodism has declined among the laity, attempts have and are still being made to recover these pristine values. The Methodist Sacramental Fellowship, the liturgical and ecumenical movements, have stimulated a new interest in devotional religious discipline. The problem facing the church in its attempts to revive the ascetic tradition is that, in modern society, alternative life-styles – scientist, innovator or radical – become increasingly attractive. As contemporary 'saints' and 'prophets' – the Luther Kings and the Gandhis – become more important, the traditional incumbents of these roles may become less so. One sociologist has already noted 'the passing of the saint':[44] perhaps we might suggest that the religious ascetic too is in the process of changing his traditional role.

## NOTES

1. Because of the close resemblance between Weber's analysis of the routinization of charisma and Ernst Troeltsch's church-sect typology, the latter is a useful way of 'reading into' this theoretical introduction.

2. For this reason, Jesus is probably the clearest example of charismatic authority, especially in relation to Jewish law. The concept of charisma is often epitomized by the dictum, 'It is written . . . but I say unto you.'

3. Max Weber, *The Theory of Social and Economic Organization*, ed. and introduced by A. M. Henderson and T. Parsons, Hodge & Co. 1947, p. 334.

4. Peter Worsley, *The Trumpet Shall Sound*, MacGibbon & Kee 1968, pp. xvii–xix.

5. H. H. Gerth and C. Wright Mills, *From Max Weber: Essays in Sociology*, Routledge & Kegan Paul 1961 (4th imp.), p. 55.

6. Max Weber, *The Protestant Ethic and the Spirit of Capitalism*, Allen & Unwin 1965 (7th imp.).

7. Indeed, Weber's thesis is not concerned with overall 'causal relations' but with patterned convergences. Weber, ibid., p. 91, refers to such a causal interpretation as 'foolish and doctrinaire'.

8. Weber's distinction between pre-modern and modern capitalism is put forward in his *General Economic History*.

9. The difference between Protestantism as a permissive and as a transforming factor in the rise of capitalism has been put most cogently by S. N. Eisenstadt in *The Protestant Ethic and Modernization*, Basic Books, New York 1968, Ch. 1.

10. Weber puts forward his concept of traditional authority in *The Theory of Social and Economic Organization*, pp. 313–29.

11. See the article by Michael Hill and Peter Wakeford and the article by Bryan Turner, both in David Martin (ed.) *A Sociological Yearbook of Religion in Britain 2*, SCM Press 1969.

12. A. M. Allchin, *The Silent Rebellion: Anglican Religious Communities, 1845–1900*, SCM Press 1958, p. 38.

13. K. S. Latourette, *A History of Christianity*, Eyre & Spottiswoode 1955, p. 837.

14. The notion behind these concepts comes from E. Gellner, *Thought and Change*, Weidenfeld & Nicolson 1964, esp. ch. 2.

15. Norman Sykes, *From Sheldon to Secker*, CUP 1959, p. 168.

16. R. A. Knox, *Enthusiasm*, Clarendon Press 1950, chs. II and III.

17. W. K. Lowther Clarke, *Eighteenth Century Piety*, SPCK 1944, p. 82.

18. G. R. Balleine, *A History of the Evangelical Party in the Church of England*, Church Book Room Press 1951, pp. 6–7.

19. As an example of a nineteenth-century Anglican statement, we might quote Sabine Baring-Gould, 'On the Revival of Religious Confraternities', in Orby Shipley (ed.), *The Church and the World*, London 1866, p. 98. A more recent example is Trevor Dearing's book which is quoted below.

20. A. Skevington Wood, *The Inextinguishable Blaze*, Paternoster Press 1960, p. 16.

21. For example, see the *Report of the Proceedings of the Church Congress of 1862*, J. & H. Parker, Oxford and London 1862, p. 143, and the *Authorized Report of the Church Congress Held at Southampton, 1870*, Gutch & Cox, Southampton 1870, p. 84.

22. Particularly by stressing the apostolic succession in the office of bishop.

23. On this point see the discussion in R. Kissack, *Church or No Church*, Epworth Press 1964, pp. 44ff.

24. Weber makes it specifically clear that 'virtuoso' is used in a non-evaluative manner and he suggests that 'heroic' religiousness is a less loaded but inadequate term.

25. Quoted by M. Edwards in R. Davies (ed.), *A History of the Methodist Church in Great Britain*, Epworth Press 1965, Vol. 1, p. 44.

26. In this paper we wish to avoid becoming involved in the problem of whether Wesley's religious style was fundamentally different after the Aldersgate conversion experience. This question, while pertinent, is not central to the issues which we raise.

27. John Wesley, *Works*, London, VIII, pp. 322–4.

28. Our discussion of prudential and instituted means of grace is heavily indebted to A. R. George, 'Private Devotion in the Methodist Tradition', *Studia Liturgica* Vol. 2, No. 3, September 1963.

29. The parallel which is drawn between Wesleyan and Tractarian devotion is connected with our treatment of virtuoso religion. See, for example, T. Dearing, *Wesleyan and Tractarian Worship*, Epworth Press/SPCK 1966.

30. In Gerth and Mills, op. cit., p. 287.

31. J. Lawson, 'The People Called Methodists; 2. "Our Discipline" ', in R. Davies (ed.), op. cit., p. 207. Although by the end of the eighteenth century ecclesiastical norms had been eroded, serious challenges had also been made to economic and social norms. In *A History of Cornish Methodism* (D. Bradford Barton Ltd., Truro 1967) T. Shaw makes the point that Cornish Methodists never, or only reluctantly, accepted Methodist injunctions against smuggling. Thus the first generation dropped religious devotionalism and the second generation dropped the Methodist norms of economic and social behaviour.

32. Southey, *Life of Wesley*, Ch. XXIX (second American edition, II, p. 308). This quotation was noted by Weber as evidence that the leaders of the Protestant movement themselves recognized the affinity between some elements of their doctrines and capitalism. See Weber, *The Protestant Ethic and the Spirit of Capitalism*, op. cit., footnotes to Ch. 5, Nos. 95, 96 & 97, p. 280.

33. For a discussion of the conflict between these polities, particularly in the nineteenth century, see J. Kent, *The Age of Disunity*, Epworth Press 1966, ch. 2.

34. R. Currie, *Methodism Divided*, Faber & Faber 1968, p. 128.

35. The following examples of class size illustrate this point:

| Period | Location | Size | |
|--------|----------|--------|------|
| | | median | mean |
| 1816 | Probus | | 18 |
| 1814 | Mansfield | 13 | |
| 1886–1905 | Spring Head (Wednesbury) | 73 | |
| 1961–6 | Connexion | | 125 |
| 1961–6 | Leeds District | | 127 |

Data on the size of class meetings from 1816 to 1905 are from Currie, op. cit., p. 128. Contemporary figures are taken from Minutes of the Methodist Conference and Synod Agendas for the Leeds District.

36. Methodist Sacramental Fellowship: 'In Defence of the Methodist Sacramental Fellowship at the Conference of the Methodist Church at Hull, 1938' (The speech of the Rev. J. E. Rattenbury, with notes), p. 12.

37. This distinction is taken from R. Stark and C. Y. Glock, *American Piety*, University of California Press 1968, p. 15.

38. John Wesley, *Works*, VIII, pp. 273–4.

39. William Pickering, 'Religion – a Leisure-time Pursuit?' in David Martin (ed.), *A Sociological Yearbook of Religion in Britain 1*, SCM Press 1968.

40. John Wesley, 'On the Duty of Constant Communion'.

41. A. R. George, op. cit., p. 234.

42. Ernst Troeltsch discusses the concept of Methodism as a religious order in *The Social Teaching of the Christian Churches*, Allen & Unwin 1931, Vol. 2, pp. 721–4.

43. See William Pickering, op. cit.

44. John M. Mecklin, 'The Passing of the Saint', *American Journal of Sociology*, Supplement to Vol. 60, May 1955, No. 6.

Secularization, Judaism and
Anglo-Jewry

*Stephen Sharot*

### Some preliminary comments on secularization

BOTH the use of the term 'secularization' and the argument that
society has become or is becoming more secular have been questioned
by a few sociologists.[1] David Martin has advocated that the term
'secularization' should be dropped from the sociologist's vocabulary
because, firstly, the secularization argument is a tool of anti-religious
ideologies; secondly, secularization has come to imply a number of
unverified, and probably untrue, propositions; and thirdly, secularization has been given a variety of meanings which are not necessarily
related in any positive way.[2]

It is true, of course, that the secularization thesis is found in the
ideologies of some anti-religious 'faiths' (Martin mentions optimistic
rationalism, Marxism and existentialism), but the thesis is also found
in pro-religious ideologies.[3] At least four positions may be delineated
regarding the association between an ideological evaluation of secularization and a belief in whether secularization has or has not occurred. The more traditional religious position, particularly that of the
Roman Catholic Church, is to evaluate negatively the secularization
that is believed to have occurred. This is also the position of some
sociologists (Will Herberg is a good example),[4] although they do not
always make their value positions explicit in their more sociological
writings. The more 'modern' theological position is to evaluate positively the secularization that is believed to have occurred. In the view
of the 'new', mostly Protestant, theologians, secularization involves
an increase rather than a loss in religiousness or religious authenticity.[5] A third position is to accept the negative connotations of what
secularization would mean but to argue that it has not in fact occurred. The critics of the secularization thesis often appear to approach
this position. Finally, a logically possible but little found position is

to accept the positive connotations of what secularization would mean but to argue that it has not in fact occurred.

The secularization thesis has been linked to a number of ideologies in a variety of ways, but this is hardly a sufficient reason for a sociologist to reject the usefulness of the term 'secularization' if he intends to use it in a value-neutral way. If a historical or contemporary linkage of a concept with one or more ideologies was regarded as a sufficient reason to drop a term from the sociologist's vocabulary, the sociologist would find he had lost many of his most important concepts. A similar argument can be made in reply to the suggestion that the term 'secularization' should be dropped because it has come to imply a number of unverified, and probably untrue, propositions, such as the incompatibility of technology and religion and the notion that secularization is unilinear and irreversible. The sociologist may simply ignore these notions or consider them as hypotheses which may or may not be true.

Finally, with regard to the third argument for dropping the term, there are no methodological advantages in rejecting the usefulness of a concept merely because it encompasses a number of dimensions which may have no positive or negative empirical relationship. In the works of Charles Glock and others the delineation of the multiple dimensions of religion (ritualistic, ideological, consequential, experiential) has led to advances in empirical research.[6] The dimensions of secularization have also been usefully delineated by both proponents and critics of the secularization thesis.[7]

I intend to use the term 'secularization' as a convenient shorthand to refer to the following two processes. Firstly, the differentiation of religious (supernatural) from non-religious (secular) perceptions or representations of the world.[8] This has been described as the disenchantment of the world-view and as a development from primitive and archaic to historical and modern patterns of thought.[9] Secondly, the differentiation of religious and non-religious roles, institutions and spheres of action. This has also been described as a compartmentalization of religion and as a decline in the relevance and number of religious actions (i.e. actions intended to communicate with or obey the wishes of supernatural beings).

Since this is not primarily a theoretical article, no attempt is made here to delineate all the possible dimensions of secularization.[10] I have chosen the two dimensions outlined above in order to present my material on Anglo-Jewry in an orderly and meaningful way. I do believe, however, that the use of these two dimensions allows for comparisons with other religious traditions while some other widely-used definitions of secularization are restricted in their applicability. The definition of secularization as a decline in the position of the church is probably limited to a discussion of Christian societies.

It is not assumed that the two dimensions of secularization used here are logically or empirically related to each other; it is possible for secularization in one dimension to occur alongside desecularization in the other. The history of Judaism shows that a radical differentiation of supernatural representations from representations of man and nature is not necessarily soon followed by a radical differentiation of religious and secular spheres of action. The attempt of the Jews to carry out the will of the transcendental God in a non-sacred world involved a pervasiveness of religious ritual in all spheres of life.

Most discussion over whether secularization has or has not occurred has been limited to a consideration of the western Christian nations. With reference to our two dimensions, we shall now consider those arguments which suggest that secularization has not occurred and that the western developed nations are not secular societies.

In reply to the thesis that the world-view of western societies has become disenchanted, the critics have maintained that it is not meaningful to refer to modern societies as secular because non-rational and superstitious thinking is widespread throughout the populations.[11]

This argument exemplifies a common tendency among the anti-secularization critics to use an absolute rather than a relative or comparative criterion in judging whether a society is secular or not. It is apparent that no society may be called 'secular' if one means by the term that religious and superstitious thinking is completely absent among the majority of the population, but it is meaningful to refer to many western societies as secular *in comparison* with former times and other contemporary societies. The time span usually considered by both the proponents and critics of the secularization thesis runs either from the high middle ages or the Victorian era to the present day. If one takes a longer time span and traces the development of certain societies from the primitive and archaic to the historical and modern, there can be little doubt that there has been a secularization of world-views.[12] Archaic and magical representations may remain important among a large proportion of a population even after a historical religion has become the 'official' religion, but the comparatively disenchanted world-view of the historical form is likely to have some influence on the masses, and the fact that the historical form is accepted as legitimate by at least some groups does constitute a secular trend.

A frequent implication in the criticisms of the secularization thesis is that the absence of a rational, empirical outlook of the majority is a sufficient reason to reject the thesis. However, a decline in the number and pervasiveness of religious (supernatural) representations may not necessarily be paralleled by a decline in irrational and non-rational representations or actions. It is possible both to disbelieve in the supernatural and be quite irrational or even non-rational in one's thinking. But although an increase in rational thinking is not a necessary part of the secularization thesis, it is possible to make a strong case that the rational, instrumentally-oriented organizations of modern industrial society do have some effect on the representations and orientations of, at the very least, their centrally located participants. If this was not so, it would be difficult to imagine how the modern bureaucratic organizations could function at all. It has been argued that science and technology are so compartmentalized in modern societies that they have had little direct effect on religious beliefs. But to argue that science and technology are compartmentalized involves the admission that religion is also compartmentalized; the effect of science may have been slight on the religious representations associated with the more private sectors of society, but its effects have been great on the economic and political sectors of society.

Closely related to the point that modern societies are not secular because the majority of their populations are not rational is the argument that the societies are not secular because there are even religious elements in the anti-religious positions of the so-called secular 'faiths' of the intellectuals. Martin, for example, suggests that there are continuities between Christianity and the anti-religious utopian ideologies (Marxism, scientism etc.), although he regards these ideologies as more simplistic and historicist (in the Popperian sense) than the ideologies of the religious tradition.[13] But even if we accept the very debatable point that there are direct continuities between religious and anti-religious ideologies, the secularization thesis is still not affected. The argument that secularization has not occurred because 'secular religions' have replaced 'non-secular religions' follows from a functional rather than a substantive definition of religion. It is possible that Christianity and Marxism (or any other secular ideology) have some similar functions, but this is a matter of empirical research and it should not be presupposed by subsuming them under a common definition. Melford E. Spiro has pointed out that supernatural beings may not necessarily be objects of ultimate concern while non-religious beliefs may sometimes be of ultimate concern. If the term 'sacred' refers to objects and beliefs of ultimate concern then sacred beliefs are not necessarily religious beliefs and profane beliefs are not necessarily secular beliefs. The sacred/profane division and the religious/secular division are regarded here as two distinct dichotomies.[14] Thus, to say that a society is secular is not to infer that its population is less concerned with ultimate problems or has fewer sacred beliefs; it means only that, in comparison with former times and other societies, the realm of the supernatural is less important.

Although it is usually admitted that there has been a differentiation of religious and secular spheres of action, some sociologists are reluctant to refer to this process as secularization. By an analogy with the family, it is argued that religion may have lost much of its relevance to many spheres of action and sectors of society but it is now able to concentrate on its 'central' or 'essential' functions. Andrew Greeley, for example, refers to the past functions of religion as 'accidental' and 'extraneous'.[15] This reasoning is obviously value-loaded; it involves an evaluation of what is an essential function of a religious institution and what is not. There is also the assumption that to correlate differentiation and secularization implies a decline in religious 'authenticity' or the ultimate value of religion. But from the point of view of a certain theological orientation a society may be both comparatively secularized and more authentically religious. The question of the importance of religion in society from a religious-value or theological perspective does not arise if the sociologist uses the term 'secularization' in the same neutral way as 'differentiation'.

Another objection to correlating differentiation with secularization is that religiously-derived ethics have become institutionalized in modern society so that more people internalize and behave in accordance with these ethics than in the past.[16] Whether most of our present day ethics were in fact derived in large part from the religious traditions is very debatable, but, even if we accept that they were so derived, their institutionalization would not affect the secularization thesis in the form that we have considered it. The important point is not the institutionalization of ethics but whether or not ethical behaviour is motivated by religious considerations or internalized through the operation of religious sanctions and rewards. An increase in ethical behaviour may be paralleled by secularization if the ethics, which may have had religious origins, are no longer internalized or performed because of a concern with supernatural sanctions and rewards or a desire simply to conform to the will of the supernatural beings.

A decline in the number and frequency of religious practices has been recorded in many European countries, including Britain, but Martin has objected to correlating this decline with secularization since a form of Protestantism devalues certain kinds of ritual behaviour.[17] Nineteenth-century Reform Judaism also maintained that 'true' religion should not be correlated with the level of performance of ritual practices. It is possible that the decline of religious practices in some countries has gone below even the minimal demands of the less ritualistic religions, but, even if this was not the case, we would argue that the decline of religious observances (i.e. acts which attempt to communicate with or obey the wishes of supernatural beings) is a neutral criterion of secularization, and that the less ritualistic religions are themselves cases of, or responses to, secularization.

The critics of the secularization thesis have corrected many exaggerations of the thesis in its cruder forms, but their polemics have sometimes led them to the other extreme of rejecting the occurrence, or even the possibility, of any secularization whatsoever. Although care should be taken not to overstate the case, there is considerable evidence to support the view that we live in a comparatively secular society.[18]

### Disenchantment and differentiation

Following the works of Max Weber, Peter Berger has recently emphasized that the roots of secularization in the West are to be found in the Old Testament in the sense that, by postulating a transcendental and historical God, Judaism broke the cosmological monism and the divine-human continuum of primitive and archaic religion. In place of the integrated sacred universe of the archaic societies, the Jews differentiated a transcendental God from a basically disenchanted world and thereby greatly extended the distance between man and the divine. The development of ethical rationalism in ancient Judaism, to which Weber gave considerable attention, involved a decline and derogation of magical representations and practices.

The disenchantment of the world-view in the West was by no means a unilinear process. Berger has pointed out that Catholicism reenchanted the world of ancient Judaism by introducing supernatural mediations between man and God, such as the incarnation, saints and the Virgin Mary.[19] Furthermore, in the folk Catholicism of the masses, the saints and the many representations of the Virgin Mary were often not worshipped because of their status as mediators with God but rather because they were believed to have relatively autonomous supernatural powers which enabled them to work directly for or against man. In some countries, the 'success' of Catholicism often meant that Catholic saints were substituted for, or syncretized with, pre-Christian gods and goddesses.[20] In such cases, the one transcendental God played only a minor role in the religious system of the masses.

There is no doubt that the one transcendental God was always prominent in the religious system of the European Jews, but it is legitimate to ask whether the world of the pre-nineteenth century Jews was quite as disenchanted as one might have supposed from a reading of the 'official' sacred texts. The evidence suggests that, at least up to the end of the eighteenth century, the world of the Jewish masses was far from disenchanted; the majority believed in saints, angels, demons, spirits and such notions as the Evil Eye and the protective power of amulets. In contrast with the unbridgeable differences between the 'legitimate' dogmas of Judaism and Christianity, many magical beliefs and practices were shared by Christians and Jews, although there were also important differences between them in this sphere.[21] Thus, although the world-view of the Jews was far more differentiated than the archaic cosmologies and probably less enchanted than the world of the 'Christian' masses, magical conceptions and 'superstitions' remained important. Furthermore, the Jewish orthodox world-view, with its radically transcendental God and world devoid of sacred qualities, was further modified by the hassidic movement which gained enthusiastic support among the Jewish masses in large areas of eastern Europe in the second half of the eighteenth century. The hassidim were pantheistic and they contributed to the enchanted view of the world by emphasizing the activity of angels and spirits down on earth. Unlike their orthodox opponents, the early hassidim believed that, since it was possible to achieve direct communion with God by ecstatic prayer, it was unnecessary to study the sacred books in order to discern the appropriate religious behaviour. At a later stage in the development of the hassidic movement, certain leading hassidim became zaddikim: saintly intermediaries between their followers and God. The charisma of the zaddic was inherited by his eldest son, although, if he did not have a son, his charisma could sometimes be transferred to a son-in-law or a principal disciple. Thus, in parts of eastern Europe in the eighteenth century, the world-view of large numbers of Jews was further desecularized.

Since the resettlement of Jews in England in the second half of the seventeenth century, the world-view of the majority of English Jews was never as religiously or magically enchanted as it was in the traditional European communities. The majority of early immigrants were Sephardim from Holland; they were wealthier, more acculturated and held more secularized world-views than the majority of European Ashkenazim. The numerical predominance of Sephardic over Ashkenazi Jews in England did not last very long, however. By 1750, approximately three-quarters of the 6–8,000 Jews in England were Ashkenazim from Holland and Germany. The immigration of poor Ashkenazi Jews rapidly increased in the second half of the eighteenth century and by 1800 the Anglo-Jewish population totalled about 25,000. The rate of immigration slowed down in the first half of the nineteenth century but began to increase again after about 1850. On the eve of the mass immigration of east European Jews, which began in 1881, the Anglo-Jewish population totalled about 50,000. In the period between 1881 and 1914, between 100,000 and 150,000 Jewish immigrants settled in England, and most came from eastern Europe.

It is unlikely that many Ashkenazi immigrants held the enchanted vision of the world which remained common in parts of eastern Europe in the nineteenth century and even later. Before 1875, the number of Jewish immigrants from eastern Europe was smaller than the number from Holland and the Germanic countries where, at least from the beginning of the nineteenth century, the Jewish world-views were comparatively secularized. As for the east European immigrants, even during the period of mass emigration, when the pogroms and economic restrictions provided forceful reasons to leave Russia, the Jews from the more traditional communities were the least likely to emigrate.[22] There were certainly very few hassidim among the east European immigrants. Hassidic immigrants were more numerous in the 1930s but they constituted a very small percentage of the Anglo-Jewish population, and by that time the hassidic world-view had become somewhat, although not extensively, disenchanted.[23]

If, since the resettlement, Anglo-Jewry has always been secular in the sense that the majority held a comparatively disenchanted view of the world, it has also always been secular in the sense that religious norms and spheres of action were differentiated from secular norms and spheres of action. In contrast to the English Jewish communities, religion was a strong determinant in the social and cultural life of the vast majority of Jews in east Europe up to about 1880 and, in large parts of eastern Europe, religion retained its importance until the destruction of the Jewish communities during the Second World War.

In the traditional eastern European communities there were few values, norms and patterns of behaviour which were completely devoid of religious content or significance, and there was almost no institution where religion was totally irrelevant. This was true for both the hassidim and their orthodox opponents (*misnagdim*). The most important value of the non-hassidic Jews was religious knowledge and their most important activities were study of the religious Law and the performance of religious rituals. It has been argued that it is difficult to find criteria for secularization in Christian societies because of the difficulty in determining those religious values and behaviours which would constitute the norms of 'religiousness'. This appears to be less a problem in Judaism where secularization may be defined as deviation from the behaviours prescribed in the Talmud and its commentaries as codified in the *Shulchan Aruch*.[24] In the traditional eastern European communities, the *Shulchan Aruch* regulated almost every act of the Jew, prescribing ritualistic observances and regulating social, business and filial relationships as well as personal regulations such as dress, diet and hygiene.

The determinacy of religion in the socio-cultural system of the eastern European Jewish communities may be illustrated by reference to the familial, educational and status systems.[25] Family activities, such as meals, were given a sacred status by the accompanying rituals; a large number of religious acts dramatized and symbolized important family events such as birth, death and marriage; and the division of roles and relationships of the family members were religiously defined and prescribed.

Although elementary arithmetic was sometimes taught, education was generally synonymous with religious education. The majority of Jewish boys attended the *chederim* (schools) where they first learnt to read and write Hebrew and Yiddish and then went on to study the Pentateuch and Talmud. The major goal of the *chederim* was to turn the more capable pupils into religious scholars who, from the ages of 12 or 13, would go on to study at the community maintained *yeshiva* (advanced educational institution). Only a few men achieved the status of scholar, but a large proportion of men devoted a few hours a day or a certain day of the week to the study of the Law.

Status in the community was determined by a combination of religious learning, wealth and *yichus* (scholarship and wealth of ancestors and relatives). Ideally, and often in practice, learning was the primary status attribute and wealth was secondary. This status system was given expression and sanction in the seating arrangements during services in the synagogues. The scholars sat at the Eastern Wall, which was the most prestigeful place to sit in the synagogue, and the distance of the other worshippers to the Eastern Wall was determined by their positions in the status system.

The early post-resettlement Anglo-Jewish communities were very different from the traditional European Jewish communities described above. For most eighteenth-century English Jews religion was no longer relevant to many roles which were religiously prescribed in the traditional European communities. A large proportion of English Jews failed to perform many important religious observances such as the dietary laws and keeping the Sabbath, religious festivals and holy days. Religious knowledge was not an important status attribute; only a few studied the Torah or concerned themselves with providing their children with a religious education. No *yeshivot* were established, and the rabbi or scholar held a comparatively low rank in the stratification system.[26] The class structure was reflected in the synagogue seating arrangements, but the seating was arranged according to wealth rather than religious scholarship.

Unlike the majority of eighteenth-century European Jews, the English Jews were not organized into legally distinct communities; the legal restrictions upon them were comparatively light; they were not segregated into ghettos or special areas; they were not subject to special taxes or numerous economic restrictions; they faced a comparatively mild form of anti-semitism; and many wealthy Jews were socially accepted by the non-Jewish upper class. These circumstances, peculiar to Europe but found also in America in the eighteenth century, explain the comparatively early and rapid acculturation of English Jews to non-Jewish patterns of behaviour. The English Jews' cultural anglicization and comparatively high level of social assimilation, especially among the upper class, inevitably involved a loss in their religio-cultural distinctiveness. The Sephardim from Holland and the more prosperous Ashkenazi immigrants from Holland and

Germany had already adopted many secular values and patterns of behaviour before they emigrated to England, but conditions in England intensified the secular trends. It is difficult to estimate the level of traditional religious conformity of the majority of poor Ashkenazi immigrants, but there is little doubt that their experiences in the comparatively 'open' English society were conducive to the adoption of a more secular way of life. Thus, since the resettlement, Anglo-Jewry was a comparatively secularized community in the sense that religion had little or no relevance for most values, norms and patterns of behaviour.

### Synagogue membership

Church membership and attendance have often been taken as indices of secularization of Christian populations. I would now like to look at the trends in synagogue membership and attendance in England and consider whether they provide indices of secularization for Anglo-Jewry.[27]

In most European countries in the nineteenth century all confessing Jews were members of the corporate Jewish community organizations (*kehillot*) which, among their many functions, provided facilities for public worship. In England there were no *kehillot* and membership of the synagogues was voluntary. Thus, the proportion of English Jews affiliated to a synagogue might at first appear to be a useful index of a commitment to Judaism. However, only a very small minority of synagogue members have attended synagogue services regularly or practised many religious observances in the home.

In the eighteenth century and first three-quarters of the nineteenth century, the price of synagogue membership in London was so high that it was restricted to the upper class and wealthier elements of the middle class. In 1847, when the Jewish population in London numbered between 18,000 and 20,000, there were six synagogues in London with a total of under 2,000 seatholders.[28] In the last quarter of the nineteenth century the east European immigrants established many small synagogues or *chevrot* which charged low membership fees, but only between a third and a half of the adult Jewish males in east London belonged to a *chevra* or synagogue before the First World War. In north London about half of the adult Jewish males were affiliated to a synagogue in 1890 but, with the migration into the area of poorer Jews from east London, the proportion fell after that date. Among the predominantly native-born, middle-class Jews living in west, south-west and north-west London, the proportion of adult Jewish males affiliated to a synagogue was much higher, but the proportion fell from about 90% in 1890 to 60% in 1914.[29] The cost of synagogue membership in north London declined from about 1890 but it remained high in west, north-west and south-west London until about 1910.[30] All this suggests a strong correlation between income and synagogue membership in the areas outside east London but, among the native middle class, synagogue membership did not indicate frequent synagogue attendance or a high level of ritualistic observance. In contrast with the first generation Jews living in the Jewish milieu of the East End of London, the middle-class, native Jews living in predominantly non-Jewish areas were faced with the problem of their Jewish identity. Membership of a synagogue provided a relatively harmless (i.e. non-isolative) way of acknowledging Jewish self-identity. Furthermore, for the Victorian, middle-class, native Jews, affiliation to a synagogue was accepted as a sign of respectability just as affiliation to, or association with, a church was a sign of respectability for their middle-class Christian neighbours.

Between one-third and two-fifths of the London Jewish population was affiliated to a synagogue in 1930, and Prais and Schmool have recently calculated that 61% of the London Jewish population was affiliated to a synagogue in 1960–65. Prais and Schmool account for this rise in synagogue membership by the greater number who now join for burial rights and who are able to pay membership fees.[31] These are no doubt contributing factors but probably a more important factor has been the migration from east London to the suburbs. An examination of synagogue membership in 1930 shows that the proportion affiliated to a synagogue in west, north, north-west and north-east London was substantially higher than the proportion affiliated to a synagogue in east London. In 1930 nearly two-thirds of the Jews in the Administrative County of London lived in east London, but by 1950 the Jews in the East End accounted for less than one-tenth of the total London Jewish population. In the pre-war period the East End was a visibly Jewish area where the majority of a Jew's neighbours, work associates and friends were Jewish. In the suburbs, where the majority of the population was non-Jewish, many Jews felt a greater need to formally acknowledge their Jewish identity and attachment to the group, and the obvious way of doing this was by joining a synagogue. Furthermore, many suburban Jews joined a synagogue in order that their children could attend synagogue classes and thereby imbue a sense of Jewishness. Thus, membership of a synagogue today appears to signify more a concern with ethnic identity than a specifically religious commitment.

### Synagogue attendance and other religious observances

Although attendance at synagogue is only one of many traditionally religious practices, it does serve as one index of secularization. In the traditional European Jewish communities the majority of men attended synagogue at least once a week and a large proportion attended every day.

The 1851 religious census in England recorded that just under 3,000 Jewish worshippers attended synagogue on Sabbath morning, 29 March 1851.[32] If we accept the population estimate, based on our knowledge of the number of Jewish births, deaths and marriages, that there were about 34,000 Jews in England in 1851, then 9 % of the total Anglo-Jewish population attended synagogue on the Sabbath morning. If the number of Friday evening and Saturday afternoon worshippers are added to the morning worshippers, the percentage or index of attendance rises to 16 %. This proportion was considerably lower than the proportion of Christians who attended church the next day; the index of attendance of the total population was 40·5 % on census Sunday.[33] This difference was due to the very low Sabbath attendances of the Jews in the cities with comparatively large Jewish populations.[34] In many provincial towns with small Jewish communities the Jewish indices of attendance were on a par or even greater than the Christian indices of attendance, but in London (where one-half to two-thirds of Anglo-Jewry lived), Liverpool and Manchester the indices of attendance were 13 %, 11 % and 18 % respectively. In comparison, the Sunday indices of church attendance of the total populations in the three cities were 37 %, 45 % and 35 % respectively.

The very low Jewish attendance in the cities was probably related both to the lack of informal sanctions and social pressures in the large communities to produce religious conformity, and to the low level of observance of the large numbers of lower-class Jews who were far less numerous in the predominantly middle-class small provincial communities. By the 1840s there were few traditionalistic immigrants; the majority of lower-class Jews were second or third generation, and many of them appear to have acculturated to the low religious observance patterns of the non-Jewish urban lower-class.[35] After 1850, the increase in the rate of immigration, the consequent greater density of

Jews in the first areas of settlement and the higher rate of economic mobility reversed the former tendencies of Jewish lower-class acculturation and assimilation.

As part of its religious census in London, the *British Weekly* recorded the Sabbath attendances on 23 October 1886 of the larger synagogues in London.[36] The proportion of the predominantly middle-class Jews who attended the Sabbath morning services in west and north-west London, which was the only area covered fully by the 1886 census, was between 10% and 15%. However, the 1886 census did not include the attendances of the immigrant *chevrot* and small synagogues which were numerous in the East End by that date.

The high level of religious observance of the east European immigrants has often been contrasted with the low level of observance among the native-born Anglo-Jews, but the importance of religion among the first generation should not be over-emphasized. Towards the end of the nineteenth century many Jews in eastern Europe were beginning to reject the traditional religious way of life and an increasing number were joining the secular Zionist and socialist movements. A minority of east European immigrants were anti-religious secularists and many others, although not anti-religious, were comparatively non-religious. But if an immigrant was religiously committed at all, his religious involvement was generally greater and his religious observances more numerous than the native middle-class Jews. There was some antagonism between anti-religious secularists and the religiously orthodox in the East End and, on a few occasions, the conflict broke out into violence. In contrast, although the native Jews were secularized, almost none were secularists; the majority were at least nominally associated with the synagogue and, like the Christian middle classes, they tended to associate atheism with socialism and anarchism.[37]

The extensive religious census undertaken by Mudie-Smith and associates for the *Daily News* in 1903 recorded church attendance on an ordinary Sunday, but the enumeration of attendance 'at every Jewish synagogue in London' was undertaken on the first day of Passover which in that year fell on Easter Sunday.[38] If the total London Jewish population was between 120,000 and 140,000, then about one in five attended synagogue on the day. Even if the one or two thousand Jews who worshipped in small *chevrot*, not recorded by the census, are added to the total, less than one in four Jews attended. Since the proportion of Jews who attended synagogue on the first day of Passover was little more than the proportion of Christians who attended church on an ordinary Sunday in 1903, the attendance of Jews on ordinary Sabbaths must have been far lower than the attendance of Christians on Sundays. The survey found that a larger proportion of the predominantly native middle-class Jews in west and north-west London attended synagogue on the day than the predominantly immigrant Jews in the East End. This difference is largely, although not fully, accounted for by the high proportion of native Jewish women who were able to attend synagogue by leaving the preparation of the Passover meal to their servants.

There appears to have been no significant difference between immigrant and native Jews in their attendance on the High Holy Days (*Yom Kippur* and *Rosh Hashanah*); in both cases, the great majority of adult Jewish men attended synagogue. The proportion of Jewish males who attended synagogue weekly may have been a little higher in the immigrant areas but, in comparison with the traditional communities in eastern Europe, weekly attendance was very low in all areas of London.

The pattern of majority attendance on the High Holy Days and very low weekly Sabbath attendance has continued up to the present day. Krausz found that, in 1963, 13·6% of the adult Jews in Edgware attended synagogue once a week; 31·4% attended on festivals and other occasions; 42·5% attended only on the High Holy Days; and 12·5% never attended. The weekly attendance was similar both to the weekly attendance of American Jews and the weekly church attendance in England.[39] However, unlike Christian church attendance, which, among the middle class at least, has declined considerably since the reign of Victoria, the pattern of synagogue attendance in London does not appear to have changed much since the middle of the nineteenth century. If regular attendance at a house of worship is taken as an index of religiosity, the secularization of Anglo-Jewry appears to have occurred earlier than the secularization of the majority of the population.

Synagogue attendance is, of course, only one of a large number of religious observances enjoined upon the Jew. We have devoted some space to it, not because it is regarded as a more significant religious index than other observances, but because it is the only religious practice on which we have statistical information extended over a period of time. Our knowledge even of the present level of religious observances among English Jews is very scanty. The very few and limited statistical surveys that have been made[40] have found that rituals which require daily attention or are inconvenient are observed by only a small minority. Very few Jewish men put on *tefillin* (phylacteries worn during weekday morning prayers), and most Jews do not avoid riding on the Sabbath. The majority of Jewish families keep at least some of the dietary laws at home, but only a small minority abstain from eating non-kosher food outside the home. Rituals which involve voluntary segregation from the 'host' society are observed by only a minority, but other rituals, which are performed in the home and centre on the family, are observed by the majority or a large proportion. An example of a popular ritual is the lighting of Sabbath candles on Friday night. Apart from the High Holy Days, the most popular festivals are those which involve family and children celebrations such as Passover with its *Seder* night meal and *Chanukah* with its candle lighting and children's parties. The popularity of *Chanukah*, which was traditionally a minor festival, is due also perhaps to its proximity to Christmas.

The majority of English Jews continue to observe the religious rites of passage: most Jewish couples marry in synagogue; most Jews 'sit *shiva*'[41] after the death of a parent; a large proportion of Jewish men say *Kaddis*[42] every day for a year after the death of a parent; and most Jewish boys of 13 years have a *barmitzvah*. The *barmitzvah* has lost much of its significance as a religious rite of passage, and it now denotes more an end to religious obligations than a beginning; after the age of 13 most boys leave the synagogue educational classes and attend synagogue services less frequently. But the *barmitzvah* social celebration, which takes place after the religious ceremony, has grown in importance since, like wedding celebrations, it provides many parents with an opportunity to demonstrate, by conspicuous expenditure, their actual or aspired class position.

The level of religious observance of Anglo-Jewry is very low compared with the traditional European communities of the past and the small remaining traditionally-observant communities (hassidic and non-hassidic) which are found in a few areas such as Stanford Hill in London and Gateshead. But, on the available evidence, such as letters, biographies, novels and newspaper reports, the level of religious observance among the pre-World War One, middle-class, native Jews appears to have been no higher, and possibly even lower, than the level of religious observance among native Jews today. For example, the *Jewish Chronicle* reported in 1884 that 'sitting *shiva*' was observed only by 'the very poor and humbler members of the trading classes'.[43] The majority of east European immigrants observed many more religious rituals than the native Jews although, as we have already said, one should be careful not to overstate their level of observance.

Although, compared with the number of statistical surveys in America, the evidence we have to go on in England is very meagre, there can be little doubt that there has been an overall decline in the average level of religious observance from the eastern European immigrants to their children, the second generation, and from the second generation to the third. However, as we have already noted, certain rituals, such as the lighting of Sabbath candles, have remained strong, and one or two observances, such as the lighting of *Chanukah* candles, may even have increased. In a recent study of a Jewish suburban community in America, Sklare and Greenblum found that, although the observance pattern was more limited with each succeeding generation, the deviations from the parental pattern of observance were generally not as large among the third and fourth generations as among the first and second generations. They concluded that the third and fourth generations displayed a stabilization and homogenization of religious observances at a minimal level; the majority performed a very few rituals and only a very small proportion performed no rituals at all.[44] It is very probable that a similar process has been taking place among English Jews. There has certainly been a decline in Anglo-Jewry of the anti-religious secularists who were not uncommon in the pre-World War One immigrant community. Some commentators have maintained that a significant minority of the younger Jews today observe a greater number of rituals than their parents, but the evidence is very impressionistic and much research needs to be done.

### Conclusions

If a disenchanted perception of the world and a substantial differentiation of religious and secular spheres of action are taken to be indices of secularization, we may conclude that, since the resettlement, Anglo-Jewry has been a comparatively secularized Jewish population. Although many immigrants had already rejected much of the traditionally religious way of life before their arrival in England, the effect of the comparatively 'open' English society was to rapidly secularize or extend the secularization of the first generation and to further secularize their children and grandchildren. We cannot, however, talk about a unilinear trend towards secularization in Anglo-Jewry. One effect of the mass east European immigration was to extend the average religious observance pattern of Anglo-Jewry, although this again declined as the second and third generations replaced the first. The religious observance pattern of today's predominantly native-born, middle-class Anglo-Jewry appears to be no more limited than the observance pattern of the native, middle-class Jews of the Victorian era, and it is possible that the observance pattern is becoming stabilized at the present low level. As far as synagogue attendance is concerned, the pattern has changed little in the large cities since the middle of the nineteenth century, although regular attendance in the smaller provincial communities has no doubt declined.

In contrast with the traditionally religious European communities, which in some parts of eastern Europe lasted until 1939, the Anglo-Jewish population is a comparatively secularized national community but, as we have shown above, the secular nature of Anglo-Jewry is not a recent or post-Victorian development. However, if the post-resettlement Anglo-Jewish population has always been comparatively secularized, it has never been, or even come close to being, fully secularized. The vast majority of English Jews observe at least some rituals in the home and attend synagogue at least two or three times a year. The average observance pattern today may be a minimal one but the few rituals still practised by the majority have maintained their importance.

## NOTES

1. David Martin, *The Religious and the Secular*, Routledge & Kegan Paul 1970; Andrew Greeley, *Religion in the Year 2000*, Sheed & Ward, NY 1969; Larry Shiner, 'The Concept of Secularization in Empirical Research', *Journal for the Scientific Study of Religion*, 6 (Fall 1967), pp. 207–20.
2. Martin, op. cit., ch. 1.
3. Ibid., chs. 1, 6.
4. Will Herberg, *Protestant, Catholic, Jew*, Bailey Bros. & Swinfen 1955. Also see, Peter Berger, *The Noise of Solemn Assemblies*, Doubleday & Co., NY 1961.
5. Perhaps the best known expression of this in its popularized version is, Harvey Cox, *The Secular City*, SCM Press 1965 and Penguin Books 1968.
6. Charles Y. Glock and Rodney Stark, *Religion and Society in Tension*, Rand McNally & Co., Chicago 1965, ch. 2.
7. It should be mentioned at this point that the advocates for dropping the term 'secularization' have admitted that the term may be used if it is carefully defined and then consistently employed. Shiner, op. cit., Martin, op. cit., appendix.

8. Peter Berger, *The Social Reality of Religion*, Faber 1967 (original title *The Sacred Canopy*, Doubleday, NY). Thomas Luckmann, *The Invisible Religion*, The Macmillan Co., NY 1967.

9. Robert N. Bellah, 'Religious Evolution', *American Sociological Review*, 29 (June 1964), pp. 358–74.

10. For a comprehensive delineation see, Shiner, op. cit., and Louis Schneider, *Sociological Approach to Religion*, John Wiley & Sons, NY 1969, ch. 9.

11. Martin, op. cit., esp. ch. 8.

12. Berger, op. cit., ch. 5; Bellah, op. cit.

13. Martin, op. cit., ch. 3.

14. Melford E. Spiro essay in M. Banton (ed.), *Anthropological Approaches to the Study of Religion*, Tavistock Publications 1966, pp. 85–126.

It should be clear by now that I adhere to a substantive and minimal definition of religion rather than a functional one. The advantages of a substantive over a functional definition have been argued forcibly by Robertson. Ronald Robertson, *The Sociological Interpretation of Religion*, Blackwells 1970, pp. 34–47. Also see, Berger, op. cit., pp. 175–8.

15. Greeley, op. cit., pp. 82–3. Also, see Martin, op. cit., ch. 9.

16. Talcott Parsons, 'Christianity and Modern Industrial Society' in Edward A. Tiryakin (ed.), *Sociological Theory, Values and Sociocultural Change*, Collier-Macmillan 1963.

17. Martin, op. cit., ch. 4.

18. For two different expressions of this position see Berger, op. cit., and Bryan R. Wilson, *Religion in Secular Society*, Watts & Co. 1966.

19. Berger, op. cit.

20. Emilio Willems, 'Religioser Pluralismus und Klassenstruktur in Brasilun und Chile', *International Yearbook for the Society of Religion*, 1965, pp. 189–211.

21. Joshua Trachtenberg, *Jewish Magic and Superstition*, Jewish Publication Society of America, Philadelphia 1961. T. Schrire, *Hebrew Amulets*, Routledge & Kegan Paul 1966.

22. L. P. Gartner, *The Jewish Immigrant in England, 1879–1914*, Allen & Unwin 1960.

23. A recent study of the hassidim in New York found that most hassidim no longer believe in the existence of spirits and demons, but many continue to believe in the Evil Eye and the protective power of amulets against supernatural danger. Jerose R. Mintz, *Legends of the Hasidim*, University of Chicago Press 1968.

24. Shulchan Aruch. Literally – 'prepared table'. The code of Jewish laws prepared by Rabbi Joseph Caro in the sixteenth century.

25. For a detailed account of the traditional Jewish community in Europe see, Mark Zborowski and Elizabeth Herzog, *Life Is With People: The Culture of the Shtetl*, Bailey Bros. & Swinfen 1962, and Jacob Katz, *Tradition and Crisis: Jewish Society at the End of the Middle Ages*, Collier-Macmillan 1961.

26. For a more extensive treatment of the social aspects of religious change in Anglo-Jewry since the resettlement see my D.Phil thesis, 'The social determinants in the religious practices and organization of Anglo-Jewry with special reference to the United Synagogue', Oxford 1968.

27. Secularization as reflected in the modifications in synagogue ritual are not dealt with here. I deal with this aspect in detail in my thesis.

28. *Jewish Chronicle*, 23 July 1847.

29. These are only very approximate figures. The number of synagogue members in most areas in London outside the East End is known, but the estimates of the Jewish population in the various districts are only approximate since they are calculated from the number of Jewish deaths in the areas.

30. The prices of seats in those synagogues affiliated to the United Synagogue were listed in the annual reports of the United Synagogue.

31. S. J. Prais and Marlena Schmool, 'The Size and Structure of the Anglo-Jewish Population, 1960–5', *Jewish Journal of Sociology*, Vol. X, No. 1 (June 1968), pp. 5–34.

32. 1851 Census of Worship, Public Record Office, H.O. 122. V. D. Lipman, 'A Survey of Anglo-Jewry in 1851', *Transactions of the Jewish Historical Society of England*, xvii, 1951–2.

33. Since many worshippers attended more than one service, the actual percentages of Jews and Christians who attended a place of worship must have been lower than the indices of attendance.

34. The indices of attendance of Christians were also lower in the large cities, but the differences between the indices of attendance in small towns and large cities were far greater in the Jewish population.

35. H. Mayhew, *London Labour and the London Poor*, London 1851, Vol. II, pp. 117–32. Also, see *Jewish Chronicle*, 28 December 1849.

36. *British Weekly*, Nov. 5, 12, 26, 1886.

37. For a more extensive treatment of the differences and conflicts between the native and immigrant communities see my D.Phil thesis.

38. Richard Mudie-Smith, *The Religious Life of London*, London 1904.

39. Ernest Krausz, 'A Sociological Field Study of Jewish Suburban Life in Edgware 1962–3 with Special Reference to Minority Identification', Ph.D. thesis, University of London 1965.

40. Ibid.; R. L. Henriques, 'Survey of Jewish Interests', Jewish Research Unit, London 1949.

41. Shiva – Seven days of mourning after the death of a close relative.

42. Kaddish – The mourner's prayer after the death of a close relative; usually after the death of a parent.

43. *Jewish Chronicle*, 1 August 1884.

44. Marshall Sklare and Joseph Greenblum, *Jewish Identity on the Suburban Frontier*, Basic Books, NY 1967, ch. 3.

# 9 Local and Cosmopolitan Aspects of Religious Activity in a Northern Suburb: Processes of Change

*David B. Clark*

## Locals and cosmopolitans

'OAKCROFT' is a working-class suburb on the edge of a northern industrial city. In a previous article[1] attention was focused on the religious activity of the residents in the mid-1960s and in particular on the members of the two Oakcroft Methodist churches, Wesley and Bethel.

It was observed that participants in the life of these two churches could be divided into two main types, locals and cosmopolitans. By and large the locals were to be found amongst the middle-aged and elderly members, they had been born and/or bred in the Oakcroft area and had established strong kinship ties amongst themselves. They had received a relatively short formal education, had often worked in local industries all their lives, and possessed limited ability to assimilate ideas, values and experiences which came to them from beyond their own immediate environment. In other words, they were spatially, socially and cognitively immobile. In church affairs, the locals laid great emphasis on relationships of a primary group type, regarding congregational life as very much 'a family affair' and looking to the children of members to follow their parents as the normal means of perpetuating the organization. The locals had considerable affection for 'their church' and its fabric, prized office and venerated length of service to the cause. They were bound to a set routine in ordering church affairs and still upheld, at least publicly, many of the Nonconformist mores of the late nineteenth century. Their theological stance was essentially Congregationalist and their concern with religious affairs beyond Oakcroft mainly utilitarian.

By and large the cosmopolitans were found amongst the younger members of the two Methodist churches (including in this case the young minister) and among those residents who had moved into

Oakcroft since the building of the first post-war council house estate in 1955. The cosmopolitans were linked as much by ties of friendship as kin. Quite a number had received a good formal education, often continuing their studies after leaving day school, and held white-collar jobs in the city, some with posts of considerable responsibility. They were much more open than the locals to new ideas and experiences coming from beyond Oakcroft. In the two Methodist churches the cosmopolitans were in a minority. They tended to find the family atmosphere of the church life there restrictive, being attracted more by activities which were of particular interest to them than by 'the fellowship' as such. They had little inclination to take office in the church or to commit themselves at all formally to the locally-oriented religious organization. The cosmopolitans looked on the church building as primarily having a functional importance and showed only spasmodic interest in fund raising or the maintenance of the property. They were more influenced than the locals by the new mores of the post-war era. Their stance ecclesiastically was 'non-denominational' rather than positively ecumenical, their concern with church affairs beyond Oakcroft being very limited.

The existence in Oakcroft of these *two* groups of Methodist members (though it must be emphasized that such typologies refer to the main characteristics of a number of people rather than to individuals as such) was also reflected in the other churches of the area; to the greatest extent in the Church of England, to the least extent in the Salvation Army and the Assemblies of God (where the locals completely dominated the scene). As in the previous article, however, attention here is concentrated on the two Methodist congregations, at Wesley and Bethel.

The previous article showed how the life-styles of the local and cosmopolitan churchgoers diverged in many respects. As a result tensions often arose and conflict broke out. It is the intention of this article to examine the religious activity of Oakcroft residents in the mid-1960s to see how these tensions were or were not resolved and how changes occurred in the life of the two Methodist churches. A final comment will suggest that the pattern of engagement and change which occurred is typical of much that happens in the life of the institutional church beyond Oakcroft.

### The teams

It might well be asked why conflict on the Oakcroft scene was inevitable.

Why could not locals and cosmopolitans have agreed simply to live and let live over religious matters, an attitude often found in the free and easy atmosphere of the Oakcroft public houses and working-men's clubs? As noted before,[2] this frequently happened but what prevented a permanent compromise and precipitated conflict was the arrival in the area in 1962 of a Methodist minister dedicated to establishing a more cosmopolitan pattern of church life. Whereas the cosmopolitan laity in Oakcroft not only feared to upset their locally-oriented friends but also lacked time and enthusiasm enough to engage in a protracted struggle, the minister was actually being paid as a full-time agent to lead the church in accordance with his ideals (which by his ordination had received the stamp of official institutional approval) and his training as a student both at university and theological college. He was pledged by upbringing, temperament and training to a cosmopolitan style of churchmanship and thus gave to the Oakcroft cosmopolitans the leadership, inspiration and nerve they had previously lacked. Furthermore the arrival of a cosmopolitan minister now gave that life-style rather more standing than previously in the eyes of churchgoers as well as providing sympathetic residents with a 'buffer' between themselves and their locally-oriented fellows.

Despite the appearance of a forceful cosmopolitan leader, the Oakcroft locals at Wesley and Bethel were by no means overwhelmed. They were in their turn led by several very strong personalities representing that way of life believed by many of them to be quite essential not only to their own sense of security but to the future of their churches. At Wesley, the dominant local leader was Walter Smith, just on retiring age and the third oldest of the four Smith brothers and two Smith sisters very active at that church. Walter was a widower with no children who, since the loss of his wife early in life, had at no little personal sacrifice given virtually all his spare time to the service of Wesley chapel. When he finally retired in 1965 he readily accepted the job of caretaker and general maintenance man, as well as retaining his offices as Sunday School Superintendent, Leader and Trustee. At Bethel, the outstanding and much respected leader of the locals was Ernest Brown, his numerous relatives and friends also being prominent in church affairs there. He had been until retirement in a position of some responsibility in one of the large city engineering works and though by now in his early seventies was still active and alert, spending the greater part of his time and energy in church work. He had been widowed twice and had no family. Ernest Brown had held virtually every office at Bethel and in the mid-1960s was a member of the Leaders' Meeting, the Trust treasurer and a local preacher. Behind Walter Smith and Ernest Brown stood other locals holding positions of major responsibility in their own particular church group, at Wesley the leader of the Youth Club being Walter Smith's main supporter and at Bethel the leaders of the Sunday School and the choir giving Ernest Brown faithful backing.

### Establishing the rules

The Methodist minister and his cosmopolitan sympathizers thus found themselves facing Walter Smith at Wesley and Ernest Brown at Bethel and their locally-oriented supporters. The minister and his followers were intent on trying to reshape a pattern of church life which they regarded as increasingly anachronistic, the locals on defending the *status quo* without which a most important part of their religious and social world would simply disintegrate.

Yet before the first major encounter occurred one thing was necessary to ensure that the whole engagement was not to be a non-event; agreement on both sides about 'the rules of the game'. In the case of Oakcroft, the most basic of these was the mutual understanding that neither side would defect even if disappointed with the outcome of the struggle, an understanding based on the realization that in the last resort neither could succeed without the other staying in the game. Despite the fact that the locals regarded the minister as something of a bird of passage, most of them knew that without his assistance as pastor, preacher and co-ordinator a great deal of the day-to-day work of the church in Oakcroft would soon languish. They were well aware that the minister was better placed than anyone else to represent the church in public and, despite their suspicion of cosmopolitan ways, to recruit new church members from the increasingly cosmopolitan world surrounding them. At the same time the minister and other cosmopolitans realized that they could not dispense with the locals, without whom the church would die for lack of manpower and money. With such a demise would go the departure of the minister, for lack of adequate members to contribute towards his salary, and the disintegration of the cosmopolitan forces. This interdependency, still characteristic of much of English Methodism today, was basic in determining the pattern of the conflict between cosmopolitans and locals in Oakcroft. Its relevance to the wider ecclesiastical scene will be considered more fully in a final comment at the end of this article.

Another major rule to be established was where the issues at stake were finally to be decided, that is, where ultimate authority to make decisions in church affairs binding on both sides lay. Here it was fully accepted that such authority must lie where Methodism decreed it, in the Leaders' Meeting for congregational matters and in the Trustees' Meeting for those things relating to property. The locals approved this situation because they had been brought up to use it and abide by it as the norm. The minister accepted it because if he set it aside in any major item he would be liable to answer for it in the higher councils of Methodism. From this location of ultimate authority both sides gained certain advantages. The locals gained in that a majority vote was needed in either of the two church courts mentioned above before any major changes could be made. The cosmopolitans gained in that the minister always took the chair, could arrange the agenda as he wished and could at times employ his greater knowledge of the details of the Methodist constitution to the advantage of the cosmopolitan cause.

Beyond a general agreement on both sides not to defect and to accept that authority lay in a majority verdict of the Leaders' Meeting or Trustees' Meeting, the rules were much less explicit. They were mainly fashioned by the *mores* of Oakcroft itself, a situation which initially at least gave the locals a great advantage over the minister and his cosmopolitan sympathizers, often younger and with less experience of established ways or newer on the Oakcroft scene. More than once the minister unwittingly contravened the local *mores* and was obliged by the pressure which the opposition was able to bring to bear to abandon moves in the direction of a cosmopolitan advance.

*Playing the game*

### Phase I – innovation

The Methodist minister arriving on the Oakcroft scene in 1962 began his work with certain factors in his favour. It being his first appointment, he had been stationed in Oakcroft by the Methodist Conference (i.e. he had not *chosen* to go there). Thus he came under no moral obligation to those who otherwise might have invited him to the Circuit. In fact he appeared as something of a saviour, for the Circuit to which Oakcroft belonged had not been able to find a minister ready to take up residence there as a matter of personal choice. Though probably unaware of these initial advantages the Methodist minister, against the advice of the more cautious counsel given to him in theological college, immediately launched out into a phase of innovation in the direction of a more cosmopolitan pattern of church life.

Over the first winter the minister introduced numerous cosmopolitan speakers from outside Oakcroft to address meetings on 'New Ventures in the Church', the topics covering such things as 'The Church in Industry', 'The Church on the Move – Taizé', 'The Church in the House' and 'The Church United'. In a very short time he had managed to get the Leaders at both Wesley and Bethel to accept a more cosmopolitan form of morning family service once a quarter. Within six months he had been able to establish the production of a quarterly magazine at each of his two churches; the Wesley magazine having a circulation of some 200 and being mainly in the hands of the minister and a cosmopolitan editor, the Bethel newsletter having a circulation of some 150 and being very efficiently edited by Ernest Brown, with the minister squeezing an article in when he could. But of greatest future importance (and to be mentioned more fully later) was the fact that within the first ten months the minister had initiated the establishment of the Oakcroft Council of Churches (with representatives of six churches on it) to replace the previous very *ad hoc* and infrequent co-operation between the denominations operating in Oakcroft.

During phase one (innovation) it was the charismatic impact of the new minister and the originality of his approach which helped to carry the day. The reaction of the locals to this initial cosmopolitan advance was very tentative support. In part they shared the reflected glory of a young energetic minister representing their churches on the Oakcroft scene and in part they were still ready 'to let him have his head'. The latter reaction was probably due to the locals' uncertainty as to what degree of cosmopolitan support the minister could command and to the extenuating judgment that as yet he could not be expected to know whose corns he was treading on. Thus in what is often spoken of as 'the honeymoon stage', the Methodist minister was able to take some useful initiatives in the direction of a more cosmopolitan style of church life in Oakcroft.

As mentioned above, the minister had often been told at theological college 'to make no changes in the first year'. In the light of events in Oakcroft it would seem that this can be rather dubious advice, at least regarding changes of a less than major nature. Shock tactics – provided that the rules previously referred to or their equivalent are kept – can often begin the chain reaction necessary for later large-scale changes and a fundamental shake up of a previously set pattern of life. As the description of phase two below shows it is doubtful whether 'playing the waiting game' from the start in Oakcroft would have had many additional advantages. Entering into such a traditional situation the minister and his cosmopolitan sympathizers had to do something fairly startling early on to get the game going at all.

*Phase II – infiltration*

The honeymoon stage over after about the first nine months, the local opposition began to exert a great deal more pressure on the minister and his cosmopolitan supporters to toe the line. For example, the Wesley Youth Club was run by a thoroughgoing local, a man born and bred in Oakcroft and married to the niece of Walter Smith. The minister, in his innocence assuming that the Youth Club at least would be open to cosmopolitan ideas, attempted informally to get the leader to reshape the pattern accordingly. At the next Leaders' Meeting Walter Smith, having heard all about the matter from the Youth Club, accused the minister of subversion (i.e. 'breaking the rules' by going behind his back) and persuaded the Leaders to agree that in future all suggestions concerning youth work must first go to the Youth Council (a sub-committee of the Leaders' Meeting) for approval before anywhere else. As Walter Smith dominated the Youth Council even more than the Leaders, this virtually gave him the veto over anything the minister wanted to introduce in the youthwork field.

A similar reaction was evoked at Bethel when the minister suggested to the Leaders on one occasion consideration of a Christian Stewardship scheme and on another the reduction of Sunday School Anniversary Sundays from two to one, though in these cases there was no accusation of clandestine activity. Here Ernest Brown's opinion was as usual the decisive one voiced in the meeting.

The opposition of the locals hardened at this stage for several reasons. They had by now got more of the measure of the new minister and realized that his early innovations were not mere salvoes but the first signs of a full-scale cosmopolitan offensive. They also felt that by now he must be well aware of their views and could only be pursuing his policies in conscious opposition to their style of church life. At the same time they became aware that the minister's cosmopolitan supporters were either confined to certain rather isolated groups (such as the Youth Club at Bethel and the Young Wives' Group at Wesley) and were still very much of a minority in the Leaders' and Trustees' Meetings. Even those that did attend the last two meetings mentioned could usually be silenced by the fact that outside they knew the tongues of their locally-oriented friends would soon be wagging if they stepped too much out of line. Thus at Wesley, upsetting Walter Smith was feared more than rejecting the most reasonable of suggestions put forward by the minister. For example, at one Wesley Leaders' Meeting a cosmopolitan teacher who had readily accepted the minister's suggestion that a Marriage Guidance Councillor should come and speak to her young people's class, suddenly rounded on the minister and called the whole thing 'disgusting' because Walter Smith had informed her of his disapproval of such innovations.

As the local opposition stiffened, the minister had to begin a second phase of activity directed towards change of a cosmopolitan type, called here 'infiltration'. This phase was characterized by the minister doing the hard continuous round of pastoral visitation, entering into endless conversations about past, present and future and spending much time learning the more informal rules of the game, ignorance of which, as noted before, could let him down at very crucial times. Thus whereas in phase one it was the charismatic features of the minister's leadership which dazzled, in phase two he had to depend very much more on the slow build up of support through establishing strong personal relationships. But this process had its own problems and pitfalls, for after some time the minister realized that his now much deeper knowledge of and sympathy for residents (including the more stubborn wing of the locally-oriented opposition) could make him fight shy of upsetting them. For example, over the minister's first year or two in Oakcroft he found himself on numerous occasions talking at length to Ernest Brown of Bethel about church affairs past and present. These conversations greatly increased the minister's appreciation of all that Ernest Brown had done over the years to further the devoted cause and made him very much more reticent to launch out on a plan of action which would probably destroy a good deal of what such locals had spent decades in building up.

Nevertheless the minister was sufficiently convinced that the introduction of a cosmopolitan style of organization and activity would in the long-run alone preserve the church in Oakcroft that he continued to press his policy through the personal contacts he made. He also made use of the pulpit to propagate the gospel according to the cosmopolitan interpretation, at the same time carefully selecting the occasions for his more forthright utterances so as not to make his preaching counter-productive. As noted, the Wesley magazine and, to a lesser extent, the Bethel newsletter gave him similar opportunities to present the cosmopolitan case.

By these means, and after three years in Oakcroft, the minister came to the point of being able to launch his main cosmopolitan attack. To the minister and many of his supporters the existence of two Methodist churches in Oakcroft carrying on their separate acts of worship and at some considerable cost maintaining separate premises only 300 yards away from each other was a contradiction of the intent of Methodist Union in 1932, let alone of the ecumenical movement as a whole. In addition, for the minister this situation meant that his round of administrative meetings was unnecessarily doubled.

Realizing the importance of 'the thin end of the wedge', the minister spent the first three years in Oakcroft encouraging joint activities between Wesley and Bethel. Fortunately a students' mission in 1961 had set going several joint house groups, much against the will of certain locals, and quarterly united services had been taking place for some time before the minister appeared on the scene. The cosmopolitan members backed these united ventures as well as a combined mid-week meeting and more united house groups which the minister got under way. By dint of steady pressure and quiet persuasion he even managed to get the two women's meetings to meet together once a quarter. However, the Wesley Youth Club remained intransigent and attempts at united youth work were a failure.

In the spring of 1964 the minister made a first tentative move towards the formation of one Methodist Society in Oakcroft. At each church a combined meeting of Leaders and Trustees (combined by the minister in order to make it harder for one church court to veto a decision made by the other on this issue) was convened. The minister was able to get the establishment of a Wesley–Bethel committee which 'in view of the changing pattern of community life and the growing population in the Oakcroft area' was briefed 'to explore ways in which the Methodist church could best meet this new situation'. At the two meetings of the joint committee held during the summer the minister was able to focus attention on the redundancy problem. In the autumn of 1964, therefore, it was agreed that the conversations be left for a year whilst the minister and a sub-committee investigated the possibility of erecting a new church to replace the two existing ones. On this sub-committee the minister was fortunate to have several leading cosmopolitans. The wedge was beginning to go in a little further. Being shrewd enough to realize this Ernest Brown wrote in the autumn edition of the Bethel newsletter: 'Do let us be careful lest we confuse the issue. We are not considering closing down our church in the immediate future as some pepole think. We have a strong and virile church and we are still doing a great work for the Master in the village. Don't let these "conversations" cause any of us to "ease off" in our work for our church because we are wondering what is going to happen next and if it is all worthwhile in view of the "conversations".'

This shot across the bows did not stop the ship, though for his local supporters it was a timely warning. Over the next twelve months the sub-committee found, as the minister expected, that the building of a new church in Oakcroft was economically quite impossible and that the only alternative was the renovation of Wesley for use by the two congregations (Bethel being on too restricted a site). The crucial question was now whether both churches would permit the minister to go ahead with enquiries about how to redesign Wesley in preparation for an eventual merger. Agreement here would mean the moral acceptance of a single Methodist Society in Oakcroft. It was a test of whether the minister's three years of personal contact and the strength of the cosmopolitans would carry the day. Early in 1966 a full meeting of all members at Bethel was held to decide the question. The locals, led vociferously by Ernest Brown, completely dominated the meeting, the cosmopolitans being virtually silent either because they still feared to expose themselves or, more likely, because they just could not bring themselves to 'take their church away from them'. In the end Ernest Brown moved that the matter 'lie on the table', only one cosmopolitan voting against and the rest abstaining. A few days later the Wesley Society Meeting accepted the Bethel resolution with regret, though it is highly doubtful whether they would have approved a move into a renovated Bethel.

Despite the fact that infiltration tactics had failed to prevent the defeat of the cosmopolitan front on what all agreed was the major issue, the minister had at least succeeded in bringing the two churches into closer contact and for a longer period than ever before. By declaring his own position with sufficient firmness yet managing the debate so that it did not become acrimonious, he was in fact able to win a good deal of sympathy, if not active support on the main issue, even from locals. Thus after his defeat, many locals were only too willing to try and 'make amends' and he was able to gain a good deal of backing for new ventures in each congregation (such as the starting of a Young Wives' Group at Wesley and the introduction of modern forms of worship at Bethel) as well as on the ecumenical front. This greatly helped him and his cosmopolitan supporters in the third phase of the engagement with the locals mentioned below.

*Phase III – circumvention*

The minister being repulsed and the cosmopolitans being forced into submission on the issue of uniting Wesley and Bethel, a third process of achieving change assumed great importance. Though here called Phase III, it had in fact begun in the first year of the minister's time in Oakcroft. If the minister had pinned all his hopes on beating the locals on their own territory and had waited for the destruction of the locally-oriented pattern of church life before initiating any cosmopolitan changes of major importance, he would have left Oakcroft with little to his credit but the remnants of what he achieved in the first phase of innovation. However, he became aware early on that the cosmopolitan attack ought to be launched both by infiltration (tap, tap, tapping at the foundations of the old edifice) and by 'circumvention' (building the new cosmopolitan pattern of church life alongside the old local one).

The first important step in the process of circumvention of the opposition was the minister's success (mentioned with reference to Phase I) in getting his own congregations and the other Oakcroft denominations to support the establishment of an Oakcroft Council of Churches. As there was a vacancy at the parish church at the time (1963–4), the Methodist minister was the only ordained person in Oakcroft and was able to use this situation to advantage in persuading the other denominations to join the Council. Fortunately when the new vicar did arrive, he turned out to be a young cosmopolitan and the ecumenical movement in Oakcroft was given further impetus. It was above all through the Council of Churches that circumvention of the locals was made possible. Whilst the normal activities of the locally oriented congregations continued, the Council was able to demonstrate in practice rather than advocate in abstract what a cosmopolitan style of Christian community could be like.

The Council of Churches (representing five denominations) was based on a distinct and compact enough area to command not only the support of numerous cosmopolitan church members but also the active interest of many other Oakcroft residents. It thus became far more than just an organization for the propagation of inter-denominational carol parties, weeks of prayer, biscuit and cheese lunches and house-to-house collections for Christian Aid (though it did these things). In 1964 and 1965 the Council organized the visita-tion of the latest and largest council house estate to go up in Oak-croft, from which effort sprang not just a large number of valuable contacts with newcomers but the house group of estate residents (non-churchgoers) mentioned in the previous article.[3] This house group met monthly for over two years under the leadership of the Methodist minister. Ernest Brown of Bethel who once visited it felt it by and large a waste of time but, despite this, it continued to flourish.

On a broader front, the Oakcroft Council of Churches was able to launch a Good Neighbour Scheme (lay volunteers giving assistance in simple ways to residents in need referred to them by welfare workers) in which numerous cosmopolitan church members partici-pated, and later a Neighbourhood Council which drew together for discussion and corporate action (for example a protest against the City Council's treatment of local residents whose homes were being demolished for redevelopment) those working in the personal and social services of the area.

Two major projects of a cosmopolitan nature deserve special men-tion. The first was in 1966 when an ecumenical 'mission' to the area was sponsored by the Council of Churches. The Methodist minister and the vicar were able to get the local churches to accept some 14 students of all denominations into the area to help them take a new look at Oakcroft and what the churches were (or were not) doing there. The students spent their days out and about in Oakcroft talk-ing to all and sundry about life today in the home, the school, the supermarket, the child welfare clinic, the public house and so forth, and then presented a long report to the local churches both encourag-ing them in what seemed to be making a useful contribution to the area and suggesting new ventures where necessary. The report was received with the greatest of interest and for a year or more it was discussed to find ways of following up recommendations. At the same time the students found hospitality in the homes of those of denom-inations other than their own, whilst many mid-day meals were taken in other Oakcroft households. At night the students ran a large number of house groups and other activities which enabled free conversation with the locals. The venture, judged by the impact on the locals and their awakened interest in much of a cosmopolitan nature that happened, was undoubtedly a success.

The second major project launched by the Oakcroft Council of Churches was an Arts Festival. This aimed to involve both churchgoers and non-churchgoers (especially the newcomers to the area) in a week-long festival of drama, music, flower show, art, local history exhibition and so on. Although the locals put up some opposition to the use of church premises by 'outsiders' (Oakcroft had no public halls and the use of church buildings was thus essential), many of them were gradually won over to support the venture and when it was held in 1967 they actively participated. So successful was it that it was repeated again in 1969.

All these things which circumvented the normal activities of the local churches represented a style of church activity unfamiliar to the majority of locals. By allowing them to retain their own locally-oriented congregational church activities, the Methodist minister and other cosmopolitans were thus able to demonstrate, often very effectively, a foretaste of things to come. At the same time many cosmopolitans themselves were gaining new insights into the potential of their Christian style of life and new courage to press on towards making it a more lasting reality.

*Phase IV – exit the catalyst*

In 1967 the Methodist minister who had been the catalyst in the situation since 1962 left Oakcroft. He was succeeded by a locally-oriented middle-aged man in average health. The latter did not try to reverse what his predecessor had begun; he simply failed to give it any very active backing. *In fact, Sadly, he was below par!*

The consequences of this new situation were two-fold. On the one hand there was some loss of cosmopolitan impetus within the Methodist ranks. It was at times difficult for the cosmopolitan laity to keep going certain of the activities now in their hands without support 'from the centre'. Thus the house group on the new estate, where communications had always been difficult to maintain, gradually petered out (but not for 18 months). On the other hand, an impressive number of other cosmopolitan activities not only continued but here and there grew in strength. Five years of exposure to cosmopolitan ideas had opened several doors which the locals found it quite impossible to shut. The joint activities between the two Methodist churches, including the combined quarterly gathering of the women's meetings, went on and the Young Wives' Group at Wesley progressed unchecked. Another activity, the Pilgrim Group at Wesley, expanded rapidly. This had begun in 1967 and was inspired by the youngest brother of the ubiquitous Smith family, the most cosmopolitan member of the group, in part as an indirect challenge to the rather limiting influence of his own locally-oriented relatives. Basing their style more on the programme of the Young Wives' Group than any other, the organizers of the Pilgrim Group began to arrange regular evenings of a social and cultural nature including trips to the city, dinner at a country pub and a week-end away at the coast. The Pilgrim Group represented the first real break in the ranks of the locals themselves and, despite the departure of the cosmopolitan minister, gained momentum over the following years. Its success demonstrated that even some of the apparently entrenched locals were rather more dissatisfied with the old ways than they had previously been willing to admit. Ecumenically the fact that the Anglican vicar was still on the Oakcroft scene did a good deal to ensure the continuance of the cosmopolitan activities of the Council of Churches, not least the 1969 Arts Festival already mentioned.

The departure of the cosmopolitan Methodist minister also took something of the sting out of the local opposition (for example, scapegoating was no longer possible) and things which had been firmly rejected before, in part because they were personally associated with him, now received more of a hearing. After three years of passive locally-patterned leadership from the new minister, even the locals were beginning to look for something a little more inspiring and many welcomed the appointment of another young minister 'with ideas' in 1970.

Nevertheless, it would be extremely misleading to give the impression that the departure of the Methodist minister in 1967 saw the locals on the point of collapse. The old ways were still deeply ingrained and there were few signs that fundamental changes (such as the merger of the two Methodist Societies) would come about even in the more distant future. What was occurring was the *ad hoc* demonstration of a cosmopolitan style of church activity in the main alongside a local one. The genuine *integration* of the two styles remained as intractable a problem as ever and the major question seemed much more one of whether the cosmopolitans could in the end weld themselves into a viable and solidary enough group to take over the reins as the locally-oriented pattern of Methodist church life very slowly lost its hold.

### Comment

The situation as witnessed in the Oakcroft of the 1960s presents many features typical of the church in other areas of England today. The general nation-wide pattern seems to be, as in Oakcroft, of a predominantly locally-oriented church struggling on perplexed as to why it is unable to establish effective contact with an increasingly cosmopolitan society. At the same time, those cosmopolitan Christians still remaining find it more and more difficult (some would say quite impossible) to adapt their own style of life to what is a precondition of full acceptance in a locally-oriented church. Thus those cosmopolitans who still care are being obliged to pursue their own Christian life style only tangentially related to that of the locals.

At the moment most of the cards would seem to be in the hands of the locals, a situation constitutionally upheld by virtually all of the major denominations. As the legal position stands at present most congregations have to depend for their survival (including fund raising and property maintenance) on a locally-oriented, immobile laity dedicated to giving a great part of their spare time to church affairs. Even on a wider level, control inevitably falls mainly into the hands of those who can spare precious time and energy – the clergy (a large number being far from cosmopolitans), the retired and (less obvious but still a potent force) married women free of family responsibilities (as a whole more local than cosmopolitan in orientation). Cosmopolitans, mobile in every way and both unable and unwilling to sink all their energies in one area or a single institution, have relatively little chance of building a sustained opposition (even if they thought it worthwhile) and of changing the system.

Here and there, however, the cosmopolitans have taken the reins. An energetic cosmopolitan minister backed by a strong cosmopolitan group has by infiltration, circumvention (or even at the stage of innovation) broken through the locally-controlled pattern of church life. There is often a crucial issue (as with the case of the merger of the two congregations in Oakcroft) where the decision, whichever way it goes, represents a point of no return. If this is resolved in favour of the cosmopolitans the way lies open to considerable and important changes.

If it is not then the cosmopolitan members will find it extremely difficult to achieve and to maintain sufficient sense of solidarity and purpose to mount another assault. They often drift away from the scene
and leave the locals to it.

The main cosmopolitan advances have occurred not only where
minister and people have formed a united front but where social
forces have weighed heavily in their favour, as in the case of new
towns or new suburbs swamping old villages. In other areas, such as
the inner city, occasional cosmopolitan breakthroughs have been
made (but often depending almost entirely on energetic cosmopolitan
ministers) mainly because the locals have succumbed to declining
manpower and economic resources. Here the innovation phase can
frequently carry the day. Yet, by and large, the style of church life in
England still remains local in orientation with the cosmopolitans
loosely attached.

As in Oakcroft, a key factor in reorienting the pattern of church life
is the attitude of the minister. Being a full-time agent he has both the
time and energy, as well as the authority, to lead the congregation one
way or the other. However, because the church situation is structured
to uphold a local style of religious life there would seem to be little
hope of change in a cosmopolitan direction within the institution as
such if a locally-oriented minister arrives on the parochial scene.

The local-cosmopolitan encounter seems most clearly demonstrated
today in English Methodism. This would appear to be due to the fact
that a fairly democratic system of ordering church affairs embraces
an ordained ministry with reasonable authority. In other denominations the inter-dependency of laity and ministry is not so obvious and
'the rules' often discriminate in favour of one or the other. For example, the parson's freehold in the Church of England (a status not
enjoyed by Methodist ministers) means that he can if he wishes
'dictate terms' to his Parochial Church Council, whilst in the Congregational and Baptist churches, for example, the authority given to the
local laity means that the minister is often regarded as employed by
his people even more than in Methodism (where the final word on
stationing a man lies with the Methodist Conference). Thus outside
Methodism the possibility of a major local-cosmopolitan conflict
(whether it be a locally-oriented laity against the cosmopolitans led
by the minister, or a cosmopolitan laity against the locals led by the
minister – the latter be it noted a very rare situation) is very much
reduced. However, this is frequently at the expense of one side or the

other playing down its participation in and thus contribution to the welfare of the whole. Thus one finds passive and sometimes quite apathetic Parochial Church Councils on the one hand, and a notable number of Congregationalist and Baptist ministers who find an outlet for apparently unfulfilled aspirations going into secular occupations, on the other. It could be said on these grounds, therefore, that Methodism (and typical of this Oakcroft Methodism) is one of the few English denominations today in which the local-cosmopolitan struggle is being waged in anything like a realistic way. Elsewhere (as in the Roman Catholic Church and the Church of England) it would seem that conflict is often being avoided or repressed, or (as in the Congregationalist and Baptist churches) being resolved by escape on the part of many ordained ministers into a cosmopolitan world. Because of this, what happens to English Methodism, and the attempt to work a system on the basis of maximum inter-dependency of laity and ordained ministry, which it stands for (at least) constitutionally and the principle of which is slowly being accepted as the hall-mark of any future church in England, may be of far greater consequence than the size of the denomination would suggest.

Finally, the situation existing in Oakcroft has particular relevance to the present state of the ecumenical movement in this country. For example, the attempt to bring the Methodist and Anglican Churches into organic unity began by an acceptance of 'the rules' – agreement about the proper constitutional procedures and which church courts had final authority in the matter. Though objection to 'the rules' was sometimes vociferous (especially within Methodism) and though defection was often threatened, it is interesting to note how few people seem to have left either denomination over the past decade simply because of the union negotiations. Initially, the idea of an Anglican-Methodist Church in England engendered a good deal of interest and even enthusiasm ('the honeymoon stage'); it being an innovation (phase one) which caught the imagination of many (mainly cosmopolitans). However, as the opposition began to consolidate and to become more aware of its own strength, the ecumenists both nationally and locally were obliged to set out upon the hard phase of infiltration (via the press, the pulpit and a host of united gatherings to discuss the matter). Unfortunately (for the ecumenists) the Methodists were already well into phase two (infiltration) before the Anglican Church had even fully come to grips with phase one (innovation). The reason may in part be that hinted at above – that Methodism is

much more open to lay participation and democratic control and thus
the whole church is felt to be immediately involved in the issue. However, the failure of 'spontaneous combustion' in both denominations
at the same time dogged the negotiations throughout; the Anglicans
still debating the matter earnestly well after the Methodists had worn
themselves out on phase two.

In July 1969, the more locally-oriented opposition brought national
negotiations for Anglican-Methodist union to a halt; by preventing
the cosmopolitans getting a sufficient majority in Convocation the
locals achieved at least a technical (i.e. according to the rules of the
game) victory. As a result, four main reactions can be observed.

First, a few cosmopolitans (through disillusionment and impa-
tience) and locals (through anxiety that union would eventually be
achieved) abandoned the game altogether, though by thus breaking
the rules they lost all authority within the institution itself. In previous eras of church history such 'rebels' have sometimes succeeded
in establishing strong splinter groups. In the secularized climate of
the present age it seems highly doubtful whether a completely separate
protest movement on the ecumenical issue alone (be it cosmopolitan
or local in emphasis) can survive for any length of time. A second
reaction is an attempt to start the whole process of change off again
and enter once more into a phase of innovation, seen for example in
the attempt (spring 1970) of the Anglo-Catholic and Evangelical
wings of the Church of England to suggest 'a better way'. But the
novelty of the quest has now worn off and any attempt to succeed
with a new scheme will have to depend entirely on a very long period
of infiltration. Thirdly, there is the continuation of the ecumenical
movement through the re-consideration of the original scheme by the
new General Synod of the Church of England. However, even if the
vote is then favourable a great deal of local opposition will still remain and attempts to make union a reality at parish level will depend
on many years of infiltrating ecumenical ideas (as the continuing
existence of two Methodist churches in Oakcroft nearly 40 years after
Methodist union shows). The final reaction is that called, in the Oakcroft case-study, 'circumvention' (phase three). This can be seen occurring where churches, whilst retaining denominational loyalties,
are more and more frequently embarking on sharing agreements and
team ministries of an ecumenical nature. More radically it can be
witnessed in the new ecumenical renewal movement known as ONE,
founded in mid-1970, and bringing cosmopolitan Christians of *all*

*[handwritten: much exaggerated!]*

denominations into a loose-knit organization intent on 'doing their own thing' wherever they happen to be and together. Circumvention is here demonstrating the practice rather than discussing the theory of the ecumenical quest.

It is extremely hard at present to know whether major change will come more quickly and be brought to a more effective conclusion through a continuing policy of infiltration of the old structures or through their circumvention (as mentioned above total separation would seem to hold little promise at this stage in English church history). What is more certain is that both infiltration *and* circumvention will have to continue concurrently for a good deal longer before the future shape of English church life clearly appears. In the meantime the hope of reaching a satisfying resolution of the local-cosmopolitan conflict would seem to depend on the ability of all involved to live with the inevitable tensions and not to abandon the struggle altogether for sheer weariness. One thing is quite obvious; that if the local-cosmopolitan conflict is evaded or avoided by either side, Christian communities of any lasting vitality will in the years ahead be rare indeed.

## NOTES

1. David B. Clark, 'Local and Cosmopolitan Aspects of Religious Activity in a Northern Suburb', in *A Sociological Yearbook of Religion in Britain 3*, ed. David Martin and Michael Hill, SCM Press 1970, pp. 45–63.
2. Op. cit., p. 62.
3. Op. cit., p. 61.

*[handwritten notes at bottom: I was 2 miles away from all this whilst a church rather more 'cosmopolitan' in outlook. Dr. Clark perhaps underrates the psychological aspects of all this & maybe gives the minister (himself) a slightly exaggerated role in initiating change! He was not always with in his initiatives & at times too directive!]*

# 10   Mormons in Britain: a Survey

*Robert Buckle*

FOR someone interested only in exceptions to the rule, the Church of Jesus Christ of Latter Day Saints would prove a fascinating study. Whereas older established churches struggle in common against decline in membership and the indifference of young people, the Mormon Church has a youthful membership and a growing one. The body has also attracted a substantial following amongst the uprooted people who inhabit new housing estates and new towns where religious attendance tends to be low. In figures, the Mormons' Membership Department claims a British following of 66,371 people as of 1966, also a continually rising membership since the beginning of the century.

To balance this picture of expansion, it might be argued that the sustained missionary efforts of the Mormon Church could only be expected to improve membership size from its small base, but the church's total membership potential could yet prove strictly limited. Whatever the truth of this, it is noteworthy that the church has faced, and faces, particular difficulties in gaining members which it has combated with some measure of success. For instance, the practice of polygamy lies like a hoary albatross about church leaders' necks. Multi-marriage has a sensationalist ring to it for people conditioned in a culture where monogamy is upheld as morally correct, and this serves to make the Mormon Church infamous to those people who know little more about Mormon practices and beliefs. This is not merely supposition, for a survey carried out in the city of Hereford, where 108 people were questioned, found that 44% of those who claimed knowledge of Mormon practices mentioned polygamy, and roughly half of these could mention little or nothing else about the church. Two in five of this group did not realize that the practice had become discontinued by 1890 and believed polygamy to be widespread among Mormons today.

The manner in which the church was founded, based as it is upon a nineteenth-century miracle, can also be thought a hindrance to its growth. The occurrence of miracles during the historical periods relative to the bible has come under critical scrutiny in recent years; the deliverance of engraved plates by an angelic prophet in 1827 is strong meat for less sceptical people, who nevertheless like to think of miracles as belonging to the misty years of the distant past, not modern scientific times. The very name used popularly – the Mormon Church – when members prefer the official title of The Church of Jesus Christ of Latter Day Saints, points to the body's isolation. It accepts the Book of Mormon as a fundamental part of its teachings whereas every other sect rejects it. Acceptance of the Book of Mormon as divinely inspired has brought, as well, disapprobation in Establishment eyes. A small example will, perhaps, support this conclusion. During the course of research, a Citizens' Advice Bureau in the West Country was visited and information about local churches requested. Amid leaflets and booklets printed for the local Christian sects, only a Church of England inspired pamphlet, 'How to deal with a Mormon missionary', gave any indication of a Mormon church in the locality. The managers of the bureau were unwilling to carry literature published by the Mormons themselves. Public libraries in many areas, according to Mormon authorities, also greet with coldness suggestions that they should purchase books written by Mormon theologians.

That their church is not regarded as respectable by outsiders is felt keenly by members of the Church of Jesus Christ of Latter Day Saints and can be assumed to have affected the response of the sample fo Mormon members to the questions I put to them. Perhaps strangely, considering events in the last century, the feeling of living amid hostility is perhaps stronger among British Mormons today than among their colleagues in America. Thomas O'Dea, in completing his survey of the Mormon Church in USA (1957),[1] commented how far a cry the present Mormon position is from that of the despised and persecuted minority, whose existence was considered a national problem and who were driven across the continent to the wastes of Utah in the middle of the last century. Today, in America, the Mormon Church is recognized to have produced figures of importance in public life, business, science, scholarship and literature. Britain, though, has no Brigham Young University nor have men emerged eminent in fields of business or scholarship who are Mormons. The church appears to be short of upper-middle-class members who might raise the status of Mormonism in the course of pursuing their various interests. Dylan Thomas, writing of his childhood thoughts,[2] which takes us back to the Welsh 1920s, speaks of his fear of 'the sinister race of Mormons' who, every night, rode on nightmares through his bedroom. Today, it is doubtful whether British people shake in such trepidation at the Mormon existence, but it appears that what Mormons regard as institutional hostility towards themselves colours their own attitudes towards the institutions of British society.

### The survey

Two broad goals lay behind the survey; to discover what first attracted members to join the Church of Jesus Christ of Latter Day Saints, perhaps after leaving other sects to do so, and to compare Mormons' attitudes to a range of social and religious questions with the attitudes of members of other churches.

My research was centred upon a full sample of the active members of the Hereford city church branch. It was possible to compare the social composition of the church branch with other church groups by means of previously published figures. As far as the opinion questions were concerned, in order to increase sample size and minimize the influence of any local peculiarities which might appear in the response of members of a single church branch, I also questioned a number of Mormons in the Glasgow area. In all, 20 questions were put to my sample, four of which were worded especially for this purpose. The remainder were the same questions as those put to other religious denominations by Gallup Polls Ltd a few years previously, and sought a comparison of response. Many readers will be familiar with this survey, published as '*Television and Religion*'[3] which, despite its specialized sounding title, concerned itself partly with churchgoers' attitudes to a variety of religio-social topics. The report distinguished between the viewpoints of active and nominal Church of England members, Roman Catholics, Nonconformists and 'Others', a mysterious grouping which perhaps contained a few Mormons but, no doubt, Buddhists and atheists as well. Some Congregationalists, Methodists etc., would probably be dissatisfied at their communal lumping as Nonconformists if they hoped for detailed results to cover their own particular group: my survey attempted to draw a meaningful comparison of Mormon attitudes with those already considered.

Following a comparative presentation of the results of my survey with those of the Gallup Polls' survey, the interesting divergences of Mormon response are discussed. It should be noted that statistics are taken from the computerized tables published by ABC Television Ltd in 1965 (some of the totals in percentages do not equal 100) and that comparative figures for other denominations relate to *regular attenders*.

## The survey results

### A THE FACTUAL BACKGROUND

*1. The ages and social class background of the sample*

Immediately striking in connexion with the age composition of the Hereford branch of the Mormon Church is the high percentage of youthful members. Active Mormons tended to be younger than active Church of England members, Nonconformists and Roman Catholics over the country as a whole.

| Age | Mormons | C of E | NCF | RC |
| --- | --- | --- | --- | --- |
| 16–20 | 30 | 19 | 12 | 15 |
| 21–24 | 22 | 8 | 8 | 14 |
| 25–29 | 7 | 3 | 6 | 9 |
| 30–34 | 14 | 6 | 10 | 13 |
| 35–44 | 3 | 13 | 11 | 19 |
| 45–49 | 7 | 17 | 11 | 13 |
| 50–64 | 17 | 21 | 27 | 12 |
| 65– | 0 | 13 | 14 | 5 |

The Membership Department of the Church, situated in Salt Lake City was, unfortunately, unable to present exact figures to show how representative the Hereford figures are of the age composition of the church in Britain as a whole. However, a general youthful bias in membership was agreed.

Employing Gallup Polls' own rating procedure for assigning social class, the following comparison of Hereford Mormons' social background with that of active Church of England members, Nonconformists and Roman Catholics over the country was drawn.

| Social Group* | Mormons | C of E | NCF | RC | Total pop. of Britain |
|---|---|---|---|---|---|
| Average Plus | 0 | 5 | 5 | 3 | 3 |
| Average | 30 | 33 | 31 | 24 | 25 |
| Average Minus | 63 | 53 | 55 | 66 | 65 |
| Very Poor | 7 | 9 | 9 | 7 | 7 |

* These four categories in order roughly correspond to
1. the upper and upper middle class;
2. the middle class;
3. lower middle and working class;
4. those on low fixed incomes such as old-age pensioners and those without regular employment.

## 2. *Previous religious affiliation*

The religious histories of members of the Hereford church proved diverse and interesting. Converts can be seen to have been drawn from seven established Christian organizations.

| | |
|---|---|
| Church of England | 30% |
| Quakers | 8% |
| Baptists | 8% |
| Christian Scientists | 8% |
| Methodists | 3% |
| Roman Catholics | 3% |
| Salvation Army | 3% |
| None | 37% |

19% of those who had no previous religious affiliation admitted to a period of atheism. 25% of previous Church of England members had been active in that church, but none of those who had come to Mormonism from other named churches considered themselves to have been active.

## 3. *The attractions of Mormonism*

Respondents were asked: 'What was it about the Mormon Church which encouraged you to become a member?'

Answers were wide-ranging. One male member, a motorcar electrician, aged 64, claimed to have become attracted to Mormonism as a result of wide psychological and philosophical reading during which time the writings of Jung had been particularly influential. He had flirted with Roman Catholicism but had not appreciated its 'ritualistic clap-trap' and had come to Mormonism as 'a sincere and simple faith'.

At another level, a 16-year-old unskilled worker could think of only church-run youth activities as having persuaded him to join.

Responses varied considerably in their length, content and detail; nevertheless, having passed through all the difficulties of quantifying and analysing material elicited by an open-ended question, it seemed possible to isolate common motivational factors which appear to have been crucial in attracting the members.

In the first place, some 26% of the sample had made first overtures to the church, taking a positive step to discover what Mormon activity existed in their area. Their interest had been aroused by reading about Mormonism (although only one-quarter of this group had read the Book of Mormon), having friends who were members or who knew about Mormonism, or a spouse or relative who had become a convert. The remaining 74% had little knowledge of, or interest in, Mormonism before missionaries called at their homes on routine rounds. 7% of the total sample were converted upon such a first missionary call. Only a few minutes' conversation with the missionaries was necessary for a former Baptist to become convinced intuitively that Mormonism was 'right', and she had made immediate enquiries about joining the church without having met the body of its members.

After initial contact had been established, the bulk of subjects had required a greater or lesser period of further contact before becoming converted Mormons.

During this period they were likely to have spent several more hours discussing the Mormon faith with the missionaries, watching films about the church and its activities in their own homes and attending church meetings in order that they might meet existing members. Reasons for their then joining the church are listed in order of their frequency of appearance in the questionnaire response.

| | |
|---|---|
| Influence of the missionaries | 40% |
| Enthusiasm for the 'way of life' Mormonism offered, which promised a purpose to living | 37% |
| A liking for the way the church was run | 29% |
| The comprehensive explanation of things given by the church | 22% |
| Intuitive insight at a stage of contact that Mormonism is right | 22% |
| Friendliness of church members | 22% |
| Something lacking in life before, a gap the church promised to fill | 19% |
| The 'modern' and 'positive' nature of Mormonism | 14% |
| Reading of the Book of Mormon | 11% |
| Youth activities | 7% |

The fifth of the sample who held that something was lacking in their previous lives are included in this category as having expressed feelings which indicated their alienation amid secular society. A 19-year-old girl talked of herself and fellow teenagers as drifting aimlessly about together before her contact with the church and her amazement at the contrasted happiness of Mormon members when she attended her first meeting. All subjects in this category appear to have been searching, some in desperation, for beliefs, activities and contacts which would serve to assuage underlying dissatisfaction and unhappiness. Where other avenues had failed, Mormonism gave a life direction. While others, who comprised the 37% appreciating 'the way of life' Mormonism offered, did not express a severe dissatisfaction with their previous existence, they similarly appreciated the explanation of life and rules for life conduct forwarded by the church.

Reading the Book of Mormon, and first-hand conviction as to its being the 'word of God' can be seen to have rated low in its influence upon respondents becoming members. Most of the sample seem to have accepted the Book of Mormon as divinely inspired on the basis of trust for the missionaries. The intuitions, which 22% claimed had convinced them of Mormonism's rightness, appeared to have been almost exclusively sparked off by a favourable atmosphere emanating from the church as a social unit rather than inspired by deep attention to the spiritual roots of the faith and certainty as to its Godly foundation.

This does not disturb church leaders, who claim that the worth of the Mormon faith is conveyed by the spirit and happiness of its members, which shines as a proof of its being the true Church of God. Happiness certainly radiated from the majority of Mormons interviewed. The words of a 19-year-old trainee teacher speak for a whole sector of those drawn from other churches, who felt re-invigorated by their contact with the Mormon community. She said: 'It had for me what no other church could offer – the priesthood and the organization of God. It is the Church, not the church of a country, or the church of a man ... it is the Church of Jesus Christ; I know it is true.'

## B  MORMON ATTITUDES

### 4. *Happiness*

Respondents were asked: 'In general, how happy would you say you are – very happy, fairly happy or not very happy?'

|                | Mormons | C of E | NCF | RC | Gen. Pop. |
|----------------|---------|--------|-----|-----|-----------|
| Very Happy     | 71      | 71     | 70  | 62  | 56        |
| Fairly Happy   | 26      | 26     | 29  | 36  | 41        |
| Not Very Happy | 3       | 2      | 1   | 1   | 3         |

Several recently-converted Mormons classed themselves as fairly happy but 'becoming happier' through their membership of the church, whereas they had not been happy previously.

### 5. *Loneliness*

Respondents were asked: 'Do you ever feel lonely – often, sometimes or never?'

|                  | Mormons | C of E | NCF | RC | Gen. Pop. |
|------------------|---------|--------|-----|-----|-----------|
| Never Lonely     | 68      | 59     | 61  | 56  | 59        |
| Sometimes Lonely | 25      | 35     | 35  | 40  | 34        |
| Often Lonely     | 7       | 5      | 4   | 4   | 7         |

## 6. *People with good influence*

Respondents were first asked: 'Which of these people do you think has most influence for good in a community such as yours – doctor, Mormon missionary/vicar/priest, school teacher, local councillor, MP?' (Mormons were given the alternative 'Mormon missionary' instead of 'vicar' or 'priest', and Gallup Pollsters allowed their respondents to pick two or more alternatives as equally and most influential for good, if they so wished.)

|  | Mormons | C of E | NCF | RC | Gen. Pop. |
|---|---|---|---|---|---|
| Doctor | 7 | 23 | 20 | 25 | 32 |
| Mormon missionary/ vicar/priest | 54 | 59 | 55 | 65 | 35 |
| School teacher | 18 | 17 | 18 | 12 | 19 |
| Local councillor | 7 | 12 | 10 | 8 | 17 |
| MP | 7 | 6 | 6 | 5 | 10 |
| Don't Know | 7 | 3 | 3 | 1 | 4 |

In addition to the 54% of Mormons who felt that their missionaries had most influence for good, a further 29% held that missionaries had the greatest 'potential' for good. They chose another alternative through feeling that missionaries' influence upon the community at that particular point of time was too weak for theirs to be classed the greatest general influence for good.

They were then asked: 'Do you think these people do their job mainly because of the good they can do for the community, or mainly because of what they can get out of the job personally?'

| Doctor | Mormons | C of E | NCF | RC | Gen. Pop. |
|---|---|---|---|---|---|
| Community | 57 | 63 | 52 | 60 | 54 |
| Self | 7 | 3 | 15 | 8 | 9 |
| Both | 29 | 30 | 30 | 30 | 32 |
| Don't Know | 7 | 3 | 3 | 3 | 4 |

| Missionary/Vicar/<br>Priest | Mormons | C of E | NCF | RC | Gen. Pop. |
|---|---|---|---|---|---|
| Community | 100 | 80 | 76 | 85 | 67 |
| Self | 0 | 3 | 3 | 1 | 6 |
| Both | 0 | 16 | 20 | 13 | 22 |
| Don't Know | 0 | 2 | 1 | 1 | 5 |

| School Teacher | | | | | |
|---|---|---|---|---|---|
| Community | 57 | 46 | 30 | 45 | 40 |
| Self | 7 | 10 | 24 | 14 | 16 |
| Both | 29 | 39 | 40 | 35 | 37 |
| Don't Know | 7 | 5 | 6 | 6 | 6 |

| Local Councillor | | | | | |
|---|---|---|---|---|---|
| Community | 25 | 38 | 40 | 33 | 31 |
| Self | 25 | 20 | 24 | 26 | 27 |
| Both | 40 | 37 | 32 | 34 | 35 |
| Don't Know | 10 | 5 | 4 | 7 | 6 |

| MP | | | | | |
|---|---|---|---|---|---|
| Community | 7 | 37 | 31 | 27 | 27 |
| Self | 29 | 17 | 19 | 27 | 26 |
| Both | 54 | 41 | 46 | 40 | 40 |
| Don't Know | 10 | 6 | 5 | 6 | 6 |

## 7. *Religion today*

'Do you believe that religion can answer all, or most of, today's problems or not?'

|            | Mormons | C of E | NCF | RC | Gen. Pop. |
|------------|---------|--------|-----|-----|-----------|
| Yes        | 82      | 72     | 84  | 78  | 40        |
| No         | 11      | 20     | 11  | 14  | 45        |
| Don't Know | 7       | 7      | 5   | 8   | 15        |

## 8. *The importance of churchgoing*

'Do you believe a person can lead a good and useful life if he or she does not go to church?'

|            | Mormons | C of E | NCF | RC | Gen. Pop. |
|------------|---------|--------|-----|-----|-----------|
| Yes        | 61      | 90     | 87  | 78  | 94        |
| No         | 39      | 7      | 13  | 15  | 3         |
| Don't Know | 0       | 3      | 0   | 7   | 2         |

## 9. *Influence of friends*

'Speaking generally, which would you think has more influence on the way that people behave – their religion or the opinions of their friends and workmates?'

|                    | Mormons | C of E | NCF | RC | Gen. Pop. |
|--------------------|---------|--------|-----|-----|-----------|
| Religion           | 43      | 37     | 45  | 56  | 19        |
| Opinion of Others  | 57      | 49     | 45  | 44  | 65        |
| Don't Know         | 0       | 15     | 12  | 4   | 17        |

## 10. *Influence of religion on British life*

'At the present time, do you think that religion as a whole is increasing its influence on British life or losing its influence?'

|            | Mormons | C of E | NCF | RC | Gen. Pop. |
|------------|---------|--------|-----|-----|-----------|
| Increasing | 32      | 46     | 41  | 47  | 23        |
| Decreasing | 61      | 46     | 53  | 39  | 62        |
| Don't Know | 7       | 8      | 7   | 15  | 15        |

Some 64% of Mormons commented spontaneously that they felt their own church was increasing its influence, but two-thirds of these thought that this was in the face of a general religious decline.

## 11. *Classes best served by the churches*

'Whose interests do you think the different churches – Church of England, Roman Catholic, Nonconformist – look after best, or do they look after the interests of everybody equally?'

| Church of England looks after | Mormons | C of E | NCF | RC | Gen. Pop. |
|---|---|---|---|---|---|
| Upper Classes | 61 | 11 | 19 | 17 | 19 |
| Middle Classes | 25 | 9 | 8 | 10 | 12 |
| Working Classes | 0 | 2 | 2 | 3 | 2 |
| All Equally | 14 | 79 | 75 | 71 | 68 |

| Roman Catholic Church looks after | Mormons | C of E | NCF | RC | Gen. Pop. |
|---|---|---|---|---|---|
| Upper Classes | 18 | 12 | 13 | 1 | 12 |
| Middle Classes | 7 | 3 | 3 | 4 | 6 |
| Working Classes | 11 | 6 | 13 | 6 | 10 |
| All Equally | 64 | 80 | 74 | 91 | 73 |

| Nonconformist looks after | Mormons | C of E | NCF | RC | Gen. Pop. |
|---|---|---|---|---|---|
| Upper Classes | 7 | 4 | 2 | 4 | 5 |
| Middle Classes | 29 | 9 | 3 | 5 | 11 |
| Working Classes | 3 | 9 | 5 | 4 | 8 |
| All Equally | 61 | 79 | 91 | 88 | 78 |

12. 'Should the churches be mainly concerned with the spiritual life of the individual, or should they express their views on day to day social questions?'

| | Mormons | C of E | NCF | RC | Gen. Pop. |
|---|---|---|---|---|---|
| Spiritual Life | 29 | 35 | 31 | 40 | 35 |
| Social Questions | 71 | 66 | 71 | 55 | 61 |
| Don't Know | 0 | 7 | 6 | 9 | 8 |

### 13. *Neighbours*

(*a*) 'If your present neighbours moved out are there any of these you would not like to have as your new neighbour; an atheist, practising Jew, Roman Catholic, member of the Church of England, Nonconformist, someone who seldom gives religion a thought – or would you not mind any of them?'

| Would not like a neighbour who was | Mormons | C of E | NCF | RC | Gen. Pop. |
|---|---|---|---|---|---|
| Atheist | 14 | 13 | 16 | 14 | 9 |
| Practising Jew | 0 | 6 | 3 | 4 | 5 |
| Roman Catholic | 3 | 3 | 1 | 0 | 2 |
| C of E | 0 | 1 | 0 | 1 | 1 |
| Nonconformist | 0 | 1 | 2 | 0 | 1 |
| Unmindful of religion | 7 | 8 | 10 | 4 | 4 |
| Wouldn't mind any of them | 76 | 75 | 71 | 77 | 81 |

(*b*) 'Which would you most like to have as neighbour?'

| Would most like a neighbour who was | Mormons | C of E | NCF | RC | Gen. Pop. |
|---|---|---|---|---|---|
| Atheist | 18 | *1* | *2* | *2* | *2* |
| Practising Jew | 7 | *0* | *0* | *1* | *1* |
| Roman Catholic | 0 | *1* | *1* | *47* | *5* |
| C of E | 14 | *47* | *9* | *1* | *22* |
| Nonconformist | 7 | *3* | *43* | *1* | *5* |
| Unmindful of religion | 25 | *2* | *0* | *1* | *5* |
| Wouldn't mind any of them | 29 | *47* | *44* | *48* | *62* |

(Non-Mormons figures are in *italic* since direct comparison is not valid as Mormons were not given a fellow Mormon as choice of neighbour.)

57 % of Mormon preferences for a neighbour hinged upon a zeal to convert the individual who moved in next door; all 14 % of those who chose a member of the Church of England did so out of a desire to convert him.

The apparent inconsistency of 14 % rejecting an atheist neighbour while 18 % preferred an atheist is explained by the ages and lengths of church membership of individuals in the two groups. 75 % of those who greeted the thought of an atheist as neighbour with distaste were young people under 21 who thought that the presence next door of an unbeliever might weaken their own religious conviction. On the other hand, 85 % of those favourable to an atheist neighbour were mature in years and had been Mormons for at least two years. Confident in the sure foundation of their religious belief, they welcomed an atheist neighbour as a test of their conversion powers.

## 14. *Negroes*

'If you were in the USA would you support the campaign for equal rights for negroes or oppose it?'

|            | Mormons | C of E | NCF | RC | Gen. Pop. |
|------------|---------|--------|-----|----|-----------|
| Support    | 75      | 91     | 94  | 86 | 85        |
| Oppose     | 7       | 3      | 1   | 7  | 8         |
| Don't Know | 18      | 6      | 5   | 6  | 7         |

Two Mormons in the sizeable 'don't know' category said they would follow church policy, although they were doubtful if there was one or, if so, what it was. Two others claimed they would support US government policy, whatever it might be.

## 15, 16. *Homosexuals and prostitutes*

'Do you think society should condemn homosexuals (prostitutes) and punish them by law; condemn them but not punish them, or be tolerant of them?'

| Homosexuals | Mormons | C of E | NCF | RC | Gen. Pop. |
|---|---|---|---|---|---|
| Punish by law | 25 | 24 | 24 | 30 | 26 |
| Condemn, don't punish | 46 | 29 | 26 | 32 | 27 |
| Tolerate | 29 | 34 | 37 | 25 | 36 |
| Don't Know | 0 | 12 | 13 | 13 | 11 |

| Prostitutes | | | | | |
|---|---|---|---|---|---|
| Punish by law | 58 | 40 | 49 | 52 | 39 |
| Condemn, don't punish | 21 | 29 | 26 | 21 | 24 |
| Tolerate | 18 | 24 | 16 | 19 | 31 |
| Don't Know | 3 | 7 | 9 | 7 | 6 |

77% of those Mormons who believed that prostitutes but not homosexuals should be punished by law commented that prostitutes are fully responsible for their activities and are consequently the more reproachable sexual deviants. They endanger marital relationships, which are held as particularly important by Mormons through their belief in eternal marriage (the re-joining of husband and wife in heaven after death).

As was the case with members of other churches and the population as a whole, those Mormons tolerant of prostitutes were drawn chiefly from the intermediate age group (25–44).

## 17. *Multi-marriage*

Multi-marriage is practised in a number of societies in the world and some of these (e.g. Burma) are religiously devout. The question asked was: 'If multi-marriages were lawful in this country, would you favour the legislation, tolerate it, consider it sinful or don't you know?' (This question was directed only to Mormons.)

| | |
|---|---|
| Would favour it | 0 |
| Would tolerate it | 40 |
| Would consider it sinful | 43 |
| Don't know | 17 |

82% of the 'don't knows' said they would rely on 'prophets' ruling if a situation of possible multi-marriage were to come about.

## 18. *Sexual relations*

'Do you think that men and women should have sexual relations only for the purpose of having children, or should they get enjoyment out of sexual relations?'

|  | Mormons | C of E | NCF | RC | Gen. Pop. |
| --- | --- | --- | --- | --- | --- |
| Only to beget children | 29 | 8 | 12 | 29 | 9 |
| Enjoyment | 68 | 79 | 79 | 61 | 83 |
| Don't Know | 3 | 15 | 12 | 15 | 10 |

More married Mormons (74%) than unmarried (57%) believed that married couples should use sexual relations to derive pleasure.

## 19. *Religion in schools*

'What do you think the schools should do about religion; give regular religious instruction, just have scripture lessons, teach children about other religions as well as Christianity, cut out all religious teaching, or don't you know?' (Two choices allowed if the subject wished.)

|  | Mormons | C of E | NCF | RC | Gen. Pop. |
| --- | --- | --- | --- | --- | --- |
| Religious Instruction | 25 | 60 | 64 | 73 | 38 |
| Scripture lessons only | 25 | 13 | 17 | 5 | 27 |
| About other Religions | 43 | 30 | 26 | 18 | 30 |
| No religion/scripture | 7 | 2 | 0 | 2 | 4 |
| Don't Know | 3 | 4 | 2 | 8 | 8 |

One respondent commented: 'Just scripture lessons at present, but they should be modified into training under Mormon influence.' It is church policy in USA, where the Mormons run schools, to administer spiritual instruction as essential to 'the training of the whole man'. What religious instruction is given at the moment in British schools is not, of course, pro-Mormon. 11% commented that school courses which dealt with Christian belief alone threatened to arouse prejudice against other religions. Those 7% of members who believed in no religion at all in schools were young people who had recently left; they claimed that they had been turned against all religion by the lessons they had attended.

20. *Minority religions on television and radio*

'Do you think that religions with fewer followers in this country, such as Quakers or Buddhists, should appear on radio and television programmes?'

|  | Mormons | C of E | NCF | RC | Gen. Pop. |
|---|---|---|---|---|---|
| Should appear | 93 | 42 | 38 | 38 | 41 |
| Should not appear | 7 | 12 | 8 | 11 | 15 |
| Don't know | 0 | 4 | 8 | 7 | 7 |

## Discussion

The most remarkable Mormon results, hinted at in the introduction, involve members' attitudes to persons in established positions of power; MPs, local councillors and members of the established church.

|  | Mormons | C of E | NCF | RC | Gen. Pop. |
|---|---|---|---|---|---|
| MPs do their job mainly out of motives for community good | | | | | |
| Agree | 7 | 37 | 31 | 27 | 27 |
| Local councillors do their job mainly out of motives for community good | | | | | |
| Agree | 25 | 38 | 40 | 33 | 31 |
| Church of England is class-serving | | | | | |
| Agree | 86 | 22 | 29 | 30 | 33 |

Taken in conjunction, these results may be thought to express Mormon resentment at the low status afforded them by official bodies.

The cynicism of Mormons towards figures who seem to represent the establishment is not surprising considering that they themselves are outside it. They may feel the political arenas of the country full of people basically hostile to their faith. Whereas members of other churches have MPs or councillors with whom they can identify, this is almost entirely denied to Mormons. Considering the disenchantment admitted by a substantial sector of Mormons before joining the church, it is likely that they carried their cynicism into the church with them.

Writers of the Gallup Poll report commented that, even among its own members, the Church of England is regarded as more class-serving than others. More Mormons than other respondents criticized the Nonconformist and Roman Catholic churches as being class biased, but their main target of criticism was the Church of England, which was seen as the chief agent of hostility and propaganda directed against themselves.

One Mormon went so far as to claim that the Church of England looks after no interest but its own; is content to retain its wealth and established status while concerned with none outside its own hierarchy.

Mormon opinion of teachers' motives contrasts with their cynical appraisal of the former categories.

| | Mormons | C of E | NCF | RC | Gen. Pop. |
|---|---|---|---|---|---|
| Schoolteachers do their job mainly out of motives for community good | | | | | |
| Agree | 57 | 46 | 30 | 45 | 40 |

Mormons can be seen to have proved generous to teachers. The stress upon education within the Mormon Church, not only for academically-gifted young people but for older people too, may be thought to have raised the status of teaching, and some of this regard for the function is reflected in praise for individual teachers.

As regards negroes (question 14), the lower level of Mormon support for their rights of equality is probably attributable to the confused status of negroes within the church's own hierarchy and theology.

|                                                      | Mormons | C of E | NCF | RC | Gen. Pop. |
| ---------------------------------------------------- | ------- | ------ | --- | -- | --------- |
| Would campaign for negroes' equal rights in USA      |         |        |     |    |           |
| Yes                                                  | 75      | 91     | 94  | 86 | 85        |

Mormons believe that negroes bear the mark of Cain and so they endure a second-class status within the church hierarchy, being excluded from the male priesthood order. Inevitably, charges of racial prejudice have been levelled by outsiders, giving constant embarrassment to Mormon authorities. The Mormon Governor George Romney, aspirant to the Republican Party presidential nomination, was hounded by questions (from journalists) on his own and his church's racial attitudes and he disappeared early as a serious challenger. Church leaders, for their own part, deny prejudice in any sense except for preventing negroes from reaching positions in the Mormon Church in which they have authority to make decisions. This is according to prophets' ruling. A number of the British Mormon church members interviewed seemed baffled by church detail in this respect and felt unable to offer an opinion on negro rights lest it should clash with official policy. It is worth noticing that, while Mormon support for negro rights was not so great as that from other groups, an undercurrent of anti-Semitism, which the results suggest exists amid the longer-established church groups, was not evident among Mormons (question 13):

|                                     | Mormons | C of E | NCF | RC | Gen. Pop. |
| ----------------------------------- | ------- | ------ | --- | -- | --------- |
| Would not like a Jew as a neighbour | 0       | 6      | 3   | 4  | 5         |
| Would like a Jew as a neighbour     | 7       | 0      | 0   | 1  | 1         |

Those members of the general public who were referred to as believing Mormons to be polygamists to this day would perhaps be surprised to read present-day British Mormon attitudes to multi-marriage (question 17). This practice is so locked up in the American past for British Mormons that it is doubtful whether the considerations which model their response vary from those which would motivate members of other churchgoing groups.

## NOTES

1. T. O'Dea, *The Mormons*, University of Chicago Press 1957.
2. Dylan Thomas, 'Reminiscences of Childhood' in *Miscellany* (1), Dent Aldine Paperbacks 1963.
3. Social Surveys (Gallup Polls Ltd.), *Television and Religion*, University of London Press 1964.

Percentages for all demoninations other than Mormon are taken from published Gallup Poll figures, and the author accepts no responsibility for any minor inaccuracies there might be.

# 11 Bibliography of Work in the Sociology of British Religion, 1970 Supplement

## Robert W. Coles

THIS bibliography is the second supplement to a bibliography first prepared by David Martin and published in *A Sociology of English Religion*, SCM Press 1967. The first supplement was published in *A Sociological Yearbook of Religion in Britain 3*, ed. David Martin and Michael Hill, SCM Press 1970. The focus of this supplement is, as before, upon the contemporary religious situation in Britain, to which historical material is added selectively.

Necessarily, the production of these bibliographical supplements partially relies upon the co-operation of many people working within the general area of the sociology of British religion.* The directory of research in progress seems to be particularly useful in providing a service through which scholars may refer to the work of others working on similar problems, and we would welcome details from people starting research projects. In this way, the bibliography should become more comprehensive, and therefore more useful.

### 1. *General Surveys and Comments on Religion and Society*

Abercrombie, N., Baker, J., Brett, S. & Foster, J., 'Superstition and Religion: the God of the Gaps', *A Sociological Yearbook of Religion in Britain 3*, ed. David Martin & Michael Hill, SCM Press 1970

Archbishops' Commission on Church and State, Appendix D: *Church and Society*, Church Information Office 1970

Archer, Margaret Scotford & Vaughan, Michalina, 'Education, Secularization, Desecularization and Resecularization', *A Sociological Yearbook of Religion in Britain 3*, ed. David Martin & Michael Hill, SCM Press 1970

---

* I am particularly indebted to the help and encouragement I have received from David Martin, Michael Hill and Colin Campbell.

Dinwiddie, Melville, *Religion by Radio*, Allen & Unwin 1968

Gray, J., *The Social Geography of Religion in Britain*, D.Phil, Oxford 1969

Hill, Clifford, 'Some Aspects of Race and Religion in Britain', *A Sociological Yearbook of Religion in Britain 3*, ed. David Martin & Michael Hill, SCM Press 1970

Homan, Roger, 'Sunday Observance and Social Class', *A Sociological Yearbook of Religion in Britain 3*, ed. David Martin & Michael Hill, SCM Press 1970

Martin, David, 'Notes for a General Theory of Secularization', *European Journal of Sociology*, 1969, pp. 192–201

*Methodist Recorder*, Supplement, 'Church and Society', 5 November 1970

Oliver, John, *The Church and the Social Order*, Mowbrays 1968

Paul, Leslie, The Selwyn Lectures, 1969, 'Studies in the Sociology of Religion', supplement to *Colloquium* – the Australian and New Zealand Theological Review, 1969

Royds, A., 'Report on a Survey 1970', unpublished paper, Congregational Council for World Mission 1970

Wright, D. & Cox, E. *Moral and Religious Judgements of Sixth Formers: A Re-Study After Eight Years*, Research in Progress, Department of Psychology, University of Leicester

## 2. *Historical Background* (*selection*)

Battiscombe, G., 'The Church of England in the Nineteenth-Century Novel', *Crucible*, May 1969

Hall, David, J., 'Membership Statistics of the Society of Friends, 1800–1850', *The Journal of the Historical Society*, 52 (2), 1969

Harrison, Kevin, *Decline of Methodism in the Potteries between 1900–1960*, M.A. Thesis (9 St George's Avenue, Stoke-on-Trent)

Marsh, P. T., *The Victorian Church in Decline*, Routledge & Kegan Paul 1969

Marwick, William, H., 'Quakers in Victorian Scotland', *The Journal of the Friends' Historical Society*, 52 (2), 1969

Turner, B., *Methodism in Leeds, 1914 to the Present Day*, Ph.D. Thesis, University of Leeds 1970

Scott, Patrick, 'Cricket and the Religious World in the Victorian Period', *Church Quarterly*, III (2), October 1970, pp. 134–44

## 3. *Statistical Material*

Krausz, E., 'The Edgeware Survey: Demographic Results', *The Jewish Journal of Sociology*, X (1) 1968

Independent Television Authority, *Religion in Britain and Northern Ireland*, ITA Publications 1970

Paul, Leslie, 'Facing Some Basic Facts', *New Christian*, 4 September 1969

Peel, John, 'The Hull Family Survey I: The Survey of Couples, 1966', *Journal of Biosocial Science*, January 1970, pp. 45–70

## 4. *Community and Parish Studies*

Clark, David B., *Community and Suburb and Village*, unpublished Ph.D. thesis, Sheffield 1969

Clark, David B., 'Local and Cosmopolitan Aspects of Religious Activity in a Northern Suburb', *A Sociological Yearbook of Religion in Britain 3*, ed. David Martin & Michael Hill, SCM Press 1970

Jones, Vivian (ed.), *The Church in a Mobile Society*, Christopher Davis, Wales 1969

Morgan, Margaret, 'The Parish Priest and the Social Worker', *Crucible*, November 1969

Quine, Colin, *Describing and Evaluating a Consultancy Project Carried Out by Gubb* – for John Wesley Society, Oxford. Report available from 1 Whitehall Place, London, S.W.1

Schiff, Leonard, 'The Church and the Immigrant: A Note from Birmingham, England', *Crucible*, September 1969

Varney, Peter D., 'Religion in Rural Norfolk', *A Sociological Yearbook of Religion in Britain 3*, ed. David Martin & Michael Hill, SCM Press 1970

Ward, Robin H., 'Some Aspects of Religious Life in an Immigrant Area in Manchester', *A Sociological Yearbook of Religion in Britain 3*, ed. David Martin & Michael Hill, SCM Press 1970

## 5. *Priesthood and the Ministry*

Autton, Norman, *Pastoral Care in Hospitals*, SPCK 1968

Barr, Pat, 'The Evangelist', *New Society*, 2 April 1970

Batty, Margaret M., *The Contribution of Local Preachers to the Life of the Wesleyan Methodist Church Before 1932, and the Methodist Church Thereafter, in England*, M.A. thesis, Leeds 1969

Rice, Denis, 'Nuns in a New World', *New Society*, 4 June 1970

Towler, R., *An Analysis of Occupational Choice and Theological Education*, Ph.D. thesis, Department of Social Studies, University of Leeds

Turner, Bryan & Smith, David, 'The Child's View of the Minister of Religion', *Crucible*, July 1970, pp. 110–15

Wainwright, David, 'Clergy and Social Workers; Roles and Skills', *Crucible*, March 1969

## 6. *Religion and Education*

Cox, E., *Sixth Form Religion*, SCM Press 1967

Frazer-Lunn, Ann, 'God in the Laboratory', *New Christian*, 3 April 1969

Hyde, K. E., *Religion and Slow Learners*, SCM Press 1969

Wright, D. & Cox, E., *A Study of the Relationship between Moral Judgement and Religious Beliefs in a Sample of English Adolescents* and *A Re-Study After Five Years*, two unpublished papers 1970


## 7. Religion and Politics

Budge, I. & Urwin, D., *Scottish Political Behaviour*, Longmans 1966
Bochel, J. M. & Denver, D. T., 'Religion and Voting: A Critical Review and New Analysis', *Political Studies*, 18 (2), University of Dundee, June 1970, pp. 205–9


## 8. Sects and Specialized Groups

Jones, Robert Kenneth, 'Sectarian Characteristics of Alcoholics Anonymous', *Sociology*, (4) 2, May 1970
Jones, Robert Kenneth, 'Alcoholics Anonymous: A New Revivalism?', *New Society*, 16 July 1970
Krausz, E., 'The Edgeware Survey: Occupation and Social Class', *The Jewish Journal of Sociology*, XI (1) 1969
Krausz, E., 'The Edgeware Survey: Factors in Jewish Identification', *The Jewish Journal of Sociology*, XI (2) 1969
Martin, Bernice, 'The Spiritualist Meeting', *A Sociological Yearbook of Religion in Britain 3*, ed. David Martin & Michael Hill, SCM Press 1970
Wilson, B. R., 'Sectarians and Schooling', *The School Review*, 72 (1), pp. 1–21
Wilson, J., 'British Israelism: A Revitalisation Movement in Contemporary Culture', *Archives de Sociologie des Religions 26*, July–December 1968


## 9. Research in Progress

Absalom, J., *Anglo-Catholicism: Ideology and Influence*, Research in progress, M.Phil., London
Carter, D., *Social and Political Influences of Bristol Churches, 1828–1914*, Research in progress, Department of History, University of Bristol
Coles, R. W., *Patterns of Culture and Commitment in the Church of England*, Research in progress, D.Phil., University of York
Cox, Caroline *et al.*, *Inter-Denominational Study of Theological Colleges* – studying problems posed and experienced by an increasing number of named ordinands, their wives and families, Research in progress, University of Newcastle.
Dowling, W. C., *The Methodist Ministry Since Union*, Thesis research in progress, LSE
Foster, B., *A Study of Patterns of Christian Commitment*, Research in progress, University of Birmingham

Goodridge, R. M., *Comparative Religious Practice of Nineteenth-Century Bristol and Marseille*, M.Phil., Thesis in progress at LSE

Hill, M., *A Sociological Study of Religious Orders with Special Reference to Anglican Orders in the Nineteenth Century*, Research in progress, D.Phil., Oxford

Hillyer, Ruth, *The Parson's Wife*, Research in progress, M.Phil., LSE

Hinings, C. R., *The Clun Valley Survey*, Research in progress, University of Birmingham

Hunter, John, *The Society of Friends in Birmingham, 1815–1918*, Research in progress, Ph.D., Department of General Studies, Wolverhampton College of Technology

Langston, Paul, *The Determinants of the Pattern of Methodist Voting in the Unity Scheme at Circuit Level*, Research in progress, University of Keele

McCloed, D. H., *Membership and Influence of the Churches in Metropolitan London, 1885–1914*, Research in progress, Ph.D., Cambridge

Moore, R. S., *Social and Political Roles of Methodism in the Deerness Valley, 1870–1970*, Research in progress, University of Durham

Patterson, Sheila, *A Study of Migration to England*, Research in progress, Institute of Race Relations

Paul, L., *The St George's House Survey: The Role and Attitudes of the Clergy*, Research in progress, Queens College, Birmingham

Peel, John, *Hull Family Survey: Re-Study After Five Years*, Research in progress, Department of Sociology, University of York

Pickering, W. S. F., *A Sociological Study of the Place of Married Students (and their wives) in Theological Colleges in Britain*, Research in progress, Department of Social Studies, University of Newcastle

Robinson, T., *The Formation of the Church of England Board of Social Responsibility*, Research in progress, University of Sheffield

Varney, P., *The Social Geography of South Norfolk with Special Reference to Religion*, Research in progress, M.A., Durham

Whitworth, J., *Religious Utopianism*, Research in progress, D.Phil., Oxford

Wollaston, B., *Church Arrangements in New Towns*, M.A., London (projected)

Wright, D., *Different Personality Types of Religious Believer and Non-Believer*, Research in progress, Department of Psychology, University of Leicester